California's Top 10 Vacations

by Walter Houk

Armstrong Publishing Company
Los Angeles

CALIFORNIA'S TOP 10 VACATIONS
by Walter Houk

First Printing, June 1978
Copyright ©1978 by Armstrong Publishing Company
Library of Congress Catalog Card Number: 78-52684
ISBN: 0-915936-08-9
All rights reserved
Printed in the United States of America

Designed by: Duane Toutjian

Published by: Armstrong Publishing Company
5514 Wilshire Boulevard
Los Angeles, California 90036
(213) 937-3600

Table of Contents

INTRODUCTION: *A Book of Vacations*

1 SAN DIEGO PAGE 9

The city, the beach, the sea, the sun. The past still visible at Old Town, the enchanted world of Balboa Park, a reviving downtown, the romantic waterfront, the great Mission Bay aquatic park, the village of La Jolla, and ebullient Old Mexico close by.

2 SAN FRANCISCO PAGE 21

Making your way through the intense heart of The City — through Downtown, Chinatown, the Financial District, Golden Gateway, North Waterfront, and other focal points. Exploring the bay and sea edge and exploring the great park. Crossing the bridges and seeing the view.

3 LOS ANGELES PAGE 31

The city's greatest interest concentrates in two arcs reaching out from the emerging new Downtown. East up the Arroyo Seco to the great houses, museums, and gardens of the San Gabriel Valley. West along the great boulevards across the liveliest part of the city to the West Side island communities.

4 MONTEREY PENINSULA PAGE 41

Three cities project distinct personalities. Historic old Monterey, to which Cannery Row adds color. Conservative old Pacific Grove, with its butterflies and stately Victorians. Quaint, tree-softened Carmel. All on a spectacular, rock-ribbed, forested peninsula.

5 SANTA BARBARA PAGE 51

Colonial-Revival "antiquities" new in the 1920's have achieved a historic presence of their own, emphasizing a romantic cityscape in a favored Mediterranean-climate setting. Among them are Spanish and Mexican antiquities, plus beauties of landscape, shore, and sea.

6 YOSEMITE   PAGE 59

The incomparable valley, target for travelers from the world over, probably the most dramatic piece of geography in all California. See the valley and the waterfalls by tram or bike, walk some of the heights, see the giant sequoias, explore the uplands. And enjoy spring, fall, and winter.

7 PALM SPRINGS AND THE LOW DESERT   PAGE 67

The great oasis of golf, tennis, and swimming pools beguiles visitors from the East in the dead of winter, while it provides a close-in destination for millions of Californians almost the year around. But discover the fascination of the desert beyond the irrigated lawns, too.

8 GOLD COUNTRY   PAGE 75

The rolling vacation, through landscapes of unusual variety at the foot of the towering Sierra, past flourishing nineteenth-century cities and towns and ruins from more than a century ago — celebrated in legend and literature. Enjoy the old inns, the theaters, the museums, the antique shops.

9 ORANGE COUNTY FUN FACTORIES   PAGE 83

Number One and Number Two among California's fifteen theme parks are within a short distance of one another, along with another park and a scattering of museums, side shows, and assorted diversions. A concentration of this special kind of experience in one location.

10 WINE COUNTRY   PAGE 93

Another vacation region, famed in and beyond California, with a landscape unique for vineyards and picturesque wineries, old and new — along with good eating and shopping and history. And to the tours and tasting are added such grace notes as summer music, balloon rides, and hot springs.

11 TOP 10 RESORTS   PAGE 105

Your choice of small retreat or large hotel, on the beach or the coast or in a mountain valley, beside a golf course or beside a lake, perhaps out in the desert. The oldest dates from the 1880's, many are from the great resort era of the 1920's (and kept up-to-date), some are of the new generation.

12 TOP 10 SEASIDE TOWNS   PAGE 113

Another rolling vacation, with stops where the seaside ambience is appealing or the beach sings its siren song. Six are on the warm-water coast (where swimming is most agreeable) south of Point Conception, several are in northern California, one is California's only island city.

13 TOP 10 SMALL CITIES, TOWNS, AND HIDEAWAYS   PAGE 123

Try these when you want something different: the "other" Bay Area city, or the state capital, or a town so tiny it has only a 12-room antique hotel, or your own houseboat in a setting evocative of the Mississippi, or a mission town or two, a Danish enclave, a high-desert hub city.

14 TOP 10 SKI RESORTS   PAGE 137

Here are the nuts and bolts of places to ski with the most facilities in California — of which the Tahoe area is naturally dominant. Equipment is listed, along with length of the longest run, elevation (related to amount of snowfall, usually) and normal season.

INTRODUCTION: *A Book of Vacations*

THIS BOOK is not a guide in the conventional sense. It makes no attempt to list all the attractions in California.

Instead, it is a selective appreciation of a limited number of places. To bring you perspective, I have carefully sifted through the wealth of experiences and the overwhelming volume of literature that await the traveler in California.

The result is something I often have wished for myself when vacation time came around: a set of specific recommendations for places to go. And by vacation I mean a trip or visit from two weeks down to a weekend — or a three-day weekend.

All this is bound to be subjective, but I have seen enough of California and observed enough people reacting to it that I am reasonably confident of the right of each place to its listing. Even so, though the first ten chapters propose an order of rank, I wouldn't quibble if you, Dear Reader, wanted to switch some of the rankings to conform to your preferences. Here is some of the reasoning:

San Diego is placed first because of the amazing variety it offers the vacationer, including the pleasures of benign climate and location next to a colorful "foreign" country.

San Francisco comes next for its urbane values, for being the epitome of the city destination.

Los Angeles follows for being the heart of the West's major metropolis, its amorphous mantle sheltering unexpected delights.

Then comes the Monterey Peninsula, for its landscape and ambience, its atmospheric towns laced with treasures of history.

Santa Barbara is there for its mystique of place, almost unequaled in California, in an unusually favored setting.

Yosemite, of course, is without rival in the world, though its resources have been taxed by crowds.

Palm Springs is the winter resort par excellence, but its season is longer for Californians than for Eastern snow refugees, and the desert around is sometimes overlooked.

The Mother Lode offers an example of the rolling vacation through a unique district where much of the past remains visible.

Orange County's fun factories constitute a destination simply for their concentration of that particular kind of experience in an easily manageable (for the visitor) territory.

And the Wine Country creates another special-interest area vacation, a California exclusive.

Subsequent chapters take up other clusters of experience, selected as the best ten of their kind — seaside places, smaller cities and hideaways, ski centers — but not ranked in comparison with one another. You will note each location is presented alphabetically within those chapters.

There is some cross referencing, actual and implied. Some places clamor to be included among Top Ten Seaside Towns (Chapter 12), for example, but I have listed only La Jolla and Santa Barbara, with references to their chapters. Such others as Monterey and Carmel and some included in Chapter 13 seem to have other attributes more important than their seaside orientation. Again, this is a bit subjective.

And there are some seemingly obvious locations that I do not include even though they attract droves of people (or perhaps because they do). Unresolved problems of traffic congestion, crowding, air pollution, and other stresses on the environment keep them out of my Top Ten places for vacations — which is not to say they are wholly without merit, either.

As for season, there is something here for every part of the year. The desert, of course, is inhospitably hot in the summer. So are much of the Delta, the capital city, and other interior parts of California. And remember that spring and parts of summer are often gray along the coast.

Still, spring is enchanting in many parts of California, the Sierra foothills and the Gold Country, for example, and Yosemite, as it opens up and snow melt swells the streams and brings a roar to the waterfalls.

And fall is one of the marvelous sunshine seasons along the coast, in the cooling deserts, and in the Gold and Wine countries. Fall and early winter are the season of the Santa Ana, the warm wind that clears the air along the Southern California coast. And of course, the mildness of winter — in between storms — legendarily made the southern part of the state a resort for folk from less favored climes in the East.

And finally a word on nuts and bolts. Because of their ever-changing nature, I have made no attempt to clutter the text by listing dates and hours when things are open and sometimes complicated tables of admissions, room rates, transportation costs, and the like. Do your homework thoroughly in advance, assume that only a few things are free and nothing is cheap, and you will avoid disappointment.

Sails hoisted, square-rigger Star of India *looms beside Embarcadero*

Chapter 1:

San Diego

I PLACE SAN DIEGO first as a vacation destination because it has the most generous share of those physical elements—very much including the beach, the sea, the sun, and subtropical landscapes—that to me are indispensable ingredients of the successful vacation. Such change of venue may be as important as more conventional visitor attractions.

San Diego has more, of course.

There is enough of an urban scene to provide a feeling of city along with the sense of place, including the civilized pursuits of music, theater, and good dining.

There are enough visible, visitable evidences of real history to give San Diego some sense of importance in the scheme of things, starting with its role as the first European presence on the West Coast.

There is Balboa Park, with its fantasy city of the good life set amid gardens, its playing fields, its promenades, and its great zoo.

There is the perpetual allure of the waterfront and ships that sail the seas, a waterfront far more civilized than most working ports can claim.

There is the unexpectedly vast water playground of Mission Bay, an aquatic park the like of which is to be found nowhere else in the West. And there is a seemingly endless stretch of surf beach north, in the center, and south of the city.

There is La Jolla, fond memory of a more innocent day when anyone of either sufficient affluence or sufficient improvidence could fall in love with the seacoast life and leave the workaday world behind — over beyond the mist-shrouded summit of Mt. Soledad.

And there is Tijuana, ebullient neighbor like none other in America, with a touch of foreign flavor but a spirit that is not really alien.

Some highlights of these districts are set forth in this chapter, which does not attempt to be a complete catalog. But first, a note on establishing a base of operations.

Look for a place to stay among the big groupings of hotels in Mission Valley or Mission Bay. Of three other clusters, two are oriented toward San Diego Bay (on Harbor and Shelter Islands) and one consists of the urban hotels downtown — of which the newest is the elegant Little America Westgate. And in the seaside communities, La Jolla has the charming old La Valencia, and Coronado has the memorable Del Coronado (Chapter 11).

For information on accommodations and on what's going on, where to play golf, and the like, write to San Diego Convention and Visitors Bureau, 1200 Third Avenue, San Diego 92101, or telephone (714) 232-3101. For on-the-spot word, stop in at the information pavilion just off Interstate Highway 5 on the edge of Mission Bay — prominently in view and marked by signs. And *San Diego Magazine* presents monthly events and restaurant guides and a summer city guide.

Then, if you are new to San Diego, a good way to get a preliminary orientation is to take the 52-mile scenic drive. You can join it anywhere you see the white seagull route signs, which direct you along the way. The loop takes you through the most interesting parts of town, across Mission Bay and over to La Jolla, and back.

OLD TOWN AND THE HISTORY PARKS

A good place to get going is Old Town, which was actually the second phase in the development of San Diego. It has variety enough for at least half a day, which might include lunch or dinner.

Before exploring Old Town, you can walk up for an advance side trip to phase one of San Diego's history, now contained in Presidio Park, on the hill immediately above. This was the site of a Spanish *presidio* (garrison) and mission — later moved — that formed the first European settlement in California.

You will see excavations of presidio ruins, a cross built from bricks taken from the old structures, the romanticized Arthur Putnam bronzes of *The Padre* and *The Indian,* and the splendid little Serra Museum — an essay in Spanish Colonial Revival style from the 1920s. One of the most commandingly-sited buildings in San Diego, with its seaward view, it is full of mementos of the past.

Back down below, Old Town took shape in the 1820's, after the presidio disbanded and its soldiers built houses at the foot of the hill. It now comes in two parts, one owned by the State (Old Town San Diego State Historic Park), and several blocks to the east that contain antiquities amid more modern city.

At park headquarters, in a restored 1832 adobe facing the central plaza, you can pick up a map and other information. This is also the starting point for walking tours from time to time that visit restorations and reconstructions already completed: the bucolic Stewart house, the grand Estudillo town house, the rebuilt Seeley Stable (housing an antique vehicle collection), a bakery-coffee house in the Pedrorena adobe, the birthplace of the *San Diego Union* newspaper, and others.

There is also a liberal sprinkling of shops and restaurants, including one particularly lively complex called Bazaar Del Mundo, in a former motel built in the 1920's Spanish Colonial Revival style.

Outside the park boundary you'll find a candle shop in the picturesque old López adobe, a quiet adobe chapel, the tree-shaded *campo santo* (cemetery), the restored brick Whaley town house from the Victorian era, a wooden pre-fab duplex house shipped round the Horn, and other things.

Then on another hill slightly above the northeast corner of the park is Heritage Park, an unusual county refuge to which houses doomed to demolition elsewhere can be moved and restored. Four nifty Victorians on the site already are in use as office spaces — one with a period room as a museum.

BALBOA PARK: *the Prado and the Zoo*

A prominent facet of San Diego's distinctive personality is this huge and marvelous oasis in the center of the city, one of America's great parks.

One unique aspect of Balboa Park is that it may be the only place in the nation where a city has invented for itself a dreamworld past of Spanish baroque palaces and church domes and towers and plazas and Moorish gardens — of such architectural force that it has become a presence of its own.

You experience it as a small city along the Prado — the main street axis. It was built mostly in two increments for world's fairs in 1915 and 1935, and became so beloved of San Diegans that they made the temporary buildings permanent — or are in the process of so doing.

Not even Santa Barbara's similar architectural fantasies (Chapter 7) achieved such an environment, which became a cultural focus for the city. It offers the arts (theater and painting and sculpture, in galleries and garden), history and sciences (anthropology, natural history, physics, aerospace), and even play (athletic trophies and model railroad layouts).

Here you see the Old Globe and the Carter Centre Stage, both vital parts of the theater scene, the Museum of Man, the Fine Arts and Timken galleries, a great architectural lath house for shade plants, the Casa del Prado, with its theater, the Natural History Museum, the innovative space theater-science hall, and others — including a charming outdoor restaurant in the center, plus artisans, folk dancers, and a classical merry-go-round in one direction and an outdoor organ pavilion in the other.

Two monuments, the Aerospace Museum and the Old Globe Theatre were both burned in early 1978, but both had plans for reestablishment as of this writing. The Old Globe seemed likely to reappear on its same site while the Aerospace Museum was headed for larger quarters in the Ford Building, south of the Prado.

Balboa Park is a great garden, almost entirely planted from treeless hills. Inquire at the Natural History Museum about the tree and plant walks they conduct now and then, and also about narrated walks through nearby Florida Canyon — a remnant of the remarkable biotic community that once prevailed, with its Mojave yucca, barrel cactus, and other curiosities — almost miraculously spared from the dominant lawns and planted trees.

The greatest attraction of all in the park is the zoo, and if you allow half a day for the Prado area, you will probably want to spend at least equal time here (if you don't give out from park fatigue).

The zoo is a botanical garden of exotic plants from the world over as background for America's largest collection of animals: more than 5,000. Because of the mild climate, the animals do not need elaborate protection from winter cold (though penguins need refrigeration). Thus the displays are predominantly open-air.

Water lilies grace pool in front of shade plant pavilion, Balboa Park

An excellent way to orient yourself to the zoo's complexities is to take the narrated bus trip that starts just inside the entrance. You can also buy a map that outlines foot tours of one hour, two to three hours, and a full day, and you can plan alternate routes using the Skyfari — an aerial tram that takes you up above the treetops to the far side of the zoo, from which you can walk back by a variety of routes. Don't miss the Children's Zoo, an enclave with an ever-changing collection of animal babies in the nursery, an enclosure for animals for petting, and other creatures that kids (and adults) can get close to.

DOWNTOWN SAN DIEGO

The city's downtown is compact, and — except for hotels — not especially oriented to visitors. Still, I recommend a drive through.

A good sampling might start, say, at Third and B. Then proceed east on B, go south to Broadway, then west to Harbor Drive and the Embarcadero (our next visitor destination). This little loop takes you through the center of things, past some fascinating buildings from the first three decades of this century contrasting with postwar highrise towers. Some notable sights: the district where landscaping, street furniure, and signs got a unified design treatment a few years back; the superblock that houses city offices, auditorium, convention facilities, a plaza with a fountain, and a parking structure — bounded by First and Third Avenues and A and C Streets. Notice also two old theaters revived for performances: the Fox and the Spreckels.

One brief side trip gives you a look at the Gaslamp Quarter, a proposed revival of the city's Victorian-era downtown, adjacent to the present downtown. Go south on Sixth to Market, east to Fifth, then back to Broadway. You pass marvels that include some handsome restorations among the porno houses and other low-rent-district uses. It promises to be a truly fascinating district if San Diego can get its act together.

THE EMBARCADERO AND THE HARBOR

If you want to catch the romance of the sea hovering about San Diego Bay, the significant places are the Embarcadero (foot of Broadway), Harbor and Shelter Islands, and Point Loma.

The Embarcadero is more than three miles of seawall activity from the Harbor Seafood Mart on the south — with its markets, restaurants, and seaside patio — to the net-handling facilities of the fleet of giant sea-going tuna seiners on the north — long one of the most colorful "authentic" sights on the waterfront.

In between (starting from the south), you first encounter the Navy and its works. Then comes the parklike Broadway Pier — where cruise ships call and a Navy ship usually holds open house on weekends. The Harbor Cruise, at the head of the pier, offers sightseeing trips of one and two hours up and down the bay — the longer one getting out as far as the sea opposite Point Loma.

Then you pass the vessels of the Maritime Museum: a San Francisco Bay ferry, a fetching little 1904 steam yacht with a colorful history, and the towering *Star of India*. San Diego's most dramatic waterfront monument, this ship is a square-rigger and the oldest iron-hulled merchantman afloat. One admission ticket gets you aboard all three; the two larger ones are outfitted with exhibits.

Across the street, a steam locomotive and an opulent private railroad car are on display by the Pacific Southwest Rail Association.

Farther out, Harbor Island is reached by Harbor Drive opposite the airport. One of two man-made "islands" (really peninsulas created by deep-dredging the main harbor channel), it is the site of several hotels and restaurants, a marina, and a grassy strip of park favored by contemplative fishermen. All the traffic of the channel goes by, close in view. The landscaping is repeated on the mainland side of the marina in Spanish Landing Park.

Still farther, you pass the Municipal Pier — colorful with boating activity and home base for sportfishing fleet — on your way to Shelter Island. This older of the two artificial islands also houses hotels, restaurants, and marinas — along with a small fishing pier, a launching ramp for trailer boats, and a big bronze bell in a pavilion at the seaward tip — the gift of Yokohama, San Diego's sister city.

Then you drive up atop the hill hulk that runs nearly flat and due south to culminate in Point Loma, which marks and shelters the entrance to the harbor. This is the site of Cabrillo National Monument, named for the Portuguese explorer who landed on the shore below just fifty years after

Columbus discovered America. In the visitor center you will see exhibits of San Diego history and of natural history. Point Loma is interesting for its unusual plants, for the creatures of its tidal pools down below, and for the gray whales that pass close offshore every winter.

The view is grand on a clear day: out to sea, south to the Coronado Islands and mainland Mexico, east across San Diego to the mountains that form its horizon. The landmark here is a quaint old lighthouse dating from 1855. Too often obscured by low-hanging clouds, it was replaced in 1891 by a light down on the seaward shore at the foot of the cliffs.

MISSION BAY AND MISSION BEACH

From Point Loma, drive northwest and across the tidal channel of the San Diego River to Mission Bay, an aquatic park four times the size of Balboa Park. It has been under development for more than two decades, and there is still much more to come.

Home to resorts, hotels, restaurants, fishing party boat docks, marinas, and yacht clubs, it is also the site of San Diego's prime commercial tourist park: the ocean-animal showplace of Sea World — which can be a day-long outing all by itself.

Mission Bay has grassy picnic sites, sandy beaches with concrete rings where you can build a fire, still-water swimming beach, shore fishing locations, separate areas for water skiing and for sailing. Some of its specialties: a smoke house and cannery for sport fishermen, a basin for model yacht sailing and racing, the *Bahia Belle* (an excursion boat that plies between hotel docks and gets most attendance during the cocktail hour), bikeways, and such special annual events as an Easter egg hunt and a summer bathtub race (motor propelled). You can also watch sailboat and crew regattas now and then.

Mission Beach, immediately to seaward, offers surf beyond its sandy beach, in contrast to the quiet water of Mission Bay. A congested old-time beach community of houses on tiny lots, it has a combination Bohemian and affluent flavor today — as if the Mercedes were now as much at home on its streets as the bicycle — and has shops and restaurants in keeping with its outlook. As of this writing, its great old (1925) carousel and roller coaster were in danger of demolition —though defenders were rallying.

Zuñiga bronze figures dominate sculpture court at Fine Arts Gallery

LA JOLLA AND TORREY PINES

San Diego's final major treat is La Jolla, a one-time resort village that the city caught up with and absorbed, though without destroying its flavor. The village occupies the northern end of a stretch of sea-bluff coast noted for cliffs, caves, sandy cove beaches, and renowned for its waves — for board and body surfers.

The village has two main streets — Girard, perpendicular to the coast and Prospect, parallel to it — lined with shops and restaurants that give the place character. Seaward of Prospect to the west, Coast Boulevard edges a long strip of park that is La Jolla's chief amenity above the shore. North of that, street gives way to a wild, dramatic cliff-edge footpath, which returns to Prospect opposite the street called Park Row.

North of La Jolla, land falls away to a former creek-mouth lagoon site now occupied by the La Jolla Shores district. Here is a beach and tennis club from another era and a long stretch of smooth swimming beach. You can walk the beach beyond at the foot of the cliffs of Torrey Pines Mesa, but be wary of rising waters, for the beach can disappear at high tide.

Then ascending the mesa beyond, you approach the University of California, San Diego, of which Scripps Institution of Oceanography is the first unit. Stop in to see its fine aquarium. At the top of the hill, the intricate campus makes little provision for visitors — though the library is worth seeking out for its dramatic architecture.

Equally striking is the main building of the Salk Institute, farther along on Torrey Pines Road. Next to Salk is a launching area for sailplanes and hang gliders that soar on the famous Torrey Pines sea breeze updraft off the cliffs — so steady that records for length of time aloft have been set here.

Beyond, you pass golf courses, and then reach Torrey Pines State Reserve — home of the Torrey pine, one of the rarest trees (in nature) in the world. A relic from before the last Ice Age, it grows only here and on Santa Rosa Island, off the coast of Santa Barbara. Explore the trails through the forest and across bluff-top moors. In the spring you may see a coreopsis, a splash of daisylike sunshine that likewise grows here and almost nowhere else.

TIJUANA, *Next Door Neighbor*

Lastly, I would make Tijuana, which shares a boundary with San Diego, part of any San Diego vacation. It is often congested, and parts of it have certain tourist-trap aspects, but the generally pleasant dispositions of its citizens and the vitality of its street scenes make it attractive.

Note that there are several bus and tour ways to get there if you don't want to make the twenty-minute drive; inquire at your hotel.

The street named *Revolución* is the center of the tourist district from about Second to Ninth streets (the numbers are a courtesy to you, the foreigner; the streets also have names). Here are the shopping arcades, the pungent leatherwork stalls, the European import stores (the whole area operates as a duty-free port), and other emporia. And here are some of the good restaurants, Tolán — the excellent handcraft shop, and the imposing Frontón Palacio — the jai alai courts.

I also like to stroll down to the bustling Hidalgo market, two blocks east of Revolución (toward the river) on Sixth, just to enjoy the activity and the color of the bountiful fresh produce and other exotic foods. Bakeries (widely distributed) and tortilla and other food shops are also enticing.

The Tijuana action is spreading out beyond the Revolución district these days — out Boulevard Agua Caliente, for example, along which a new kind of suburban district is taking shape. There are new shops, hotels, and restaurants, in a section formerly known mainly for having the Country Club and the race track — itself now a monumental showplace with shops, restaurants, and a brandy-tasting room.

Elsewhere, new buildings are appearing in the redevelopment area along the now-channelized river. Years in the making, this is a complex of expressways, traffic circles, bridges, monuments, and landscaped or bare building sites — destined to become the heart of the city.

Golden Gate Bridge, seen from Marin County, leads to San Francisco

Chapter 2:

San Francisco

SAN FRANCISCO has been reported and analyzed enough, in my view. Its bracing climate. Its fog, to the appreciation of which natives devote considerable attention. Its resemblance to the Easterner's concept of how well-behaved cities should be structured. Its fondness for good living. Its firmly-established dedication to the traditional arts of the opera, the symphony, and the ballet. Even its faintly provincial attitude toward the world outside its 47 square miles.

I believe my mission here is to assume San Francisco is a prime vacation city destination and to concentrate on helping you grasp some of its location and street relationships.

This is not always easy. The city's greatest interest is crowded into the northeast corner of the peninsula it occupies.

And its street pattern is complicated by two quirks: First, the old street grid, angled to cardinal compass points, was replaced in the American era by an east-west, north-south grid. Thus Market Street, on the dividing line, will forever present a trauma of angles for the newcomer downtown. Then, with truly Yankee single-mindedness, the new street grid was simply imposed on some rather exciting topography, including some of the steepest of the city's forty-two hills.

So I have selected a string of districts and individual places in a swath of terrain that I hope you can visualize, or at least trace out on a map. The places described in this chapter form a rough circle along the northeast, north, and northwest edges of the city, and back, starting with a prominent focal point downtown: Union Square.

This over-simplifies, of course, and it means leaving out such fascinating places as Union Street and Alamo Square, for example. But even catalogs can't hope to list all facets of any human activity cluster as dynamic as a city, so we'll leave something for next time.

One other omission is easily rectified: restaurant selection and places to go at night. There are ample guides to the former in print, for the latter there are both newspapers and the magic telephone number: 391-2000. Dial it to hear the latest on what's happening in the city.

UNION SQUARE, *Downtown*

The downtown shopping district is the consummate image of the conventional American urban core, the sort of place where until recent years soignée ladies felt obliged to wear hats when they went in to do the shops and have lunch.

And Union Square is the heart of that shopping district, as well as of the imprecisely-bordered area called downtown. The square tops a thousand-car subterranean parking structure and the Dewey-Manila Bay monument tops the square.

Facing Union Square are two major hotels, the venerable St. Francis and the newer Hyatt. The latter's forecourt is graced by Ruth Asawa's Children's Fountain, an intricate, good-humored relief sculpture of the San Francisco story.

Around the square and nearby are the department and the specialty stores, and the sidewalk flower stands. Off it reaches the quiet, two-block-long, shop-lined Maiden Lane — with its arched, plain-brick facade storefront by Frank Lloyd Wright. The concentrated shopping section extends toward Market Street, or Kearny to the east.

Two cable car lines, Powell-Hyde and Powell-Taylor, head north along the west side of the square, over the hill to the north waterfront district (see below). These vivid links with the past often run bulging with precariously-clinging passengers. Both lines pass the antique car barn at Mason and Washington streets, which supplies motive power to the cables. You can watch the reversal of the cars at Hallidie Plaza — named for the cable cars' engineer — at the Powell-Market intersection, as well as at the far ends of the lines.

FINANCIAL DISTRICT, *Golden Gateway*

The next major quarter on our survey, the financial district melts imperceptibly into the Golden Gateway redevelopment area along its bay-ward edge. Here, new-generation tall towers have altered the scale of the skyline and the Manhattanization of the city is most apparent. One result is a street scene lively during working periods but quiet at other times.

Seen from a helicopter, the combined boundary of the adjacent areas is roughly a triangle formed by Market, Kearny, and Washington streets, with the Embarcadero cutting off one apex.

Odd corners and landscaping for buildings create little parks and public gardens, pleasant places for a rest or a brown-bag lunch: the little Mechanics Monument plaza, Zellerbach Plaza, the Standard Oil building grounds, all along Market Street. And down at the Embarcadero, a chain of parks and open space opens up, adorned by the unusual walk-through Villaincourt Fountain.

Several buildings offer public displays during working hours. One of the most notable is the Wells Fargo History Room, which includes a stagecoach. It's at 420 Montgomery, between Sacramento and California streets. The Bank of California, 400 California, has a display of "Money of the American West," and Standard Oil, 555 Market, shows "A World of Oil." And you can look in at the workings of the Pacific Coast Stock Exchange, 301 Pine, active until 2:30 P.M.

The Golden Gateway is an assemblage of new buildings, plazas, and connecting upper-level pedestrian bridges. It climaxes with one of the most exciting interior spaces built in recent years: the startlingly lofty lobby of the Hyatt Regency Hotel, near the foot of Market Street.

CHINATOWN

Walk or take the cable car up California Street from the Golden Gateway area to Chinatown. This unmistakable, colorful ethnic enclave adjoins both the shopping and the financial districts. Its two dozen or so blocks spread along the main artery, Grant Street, for two blocks south from California and six blocks north (to Broadway and Columbus). And the district extends from Kearny west to Stockton.

The cable car drops you near St. Mary's Square, a small park with parking underneath and a statue of Dr. Sun Yat Sen by San Francisco's own Beniamino Bufano. To the south at the corner of Bush is the ceremonial gate over Grant that marks an entrance to Chinatown. Bright blandishments for tourists concentrate along Grant, while food stores, restaurants, shops — including treasure-houses of Orientalia — temples, and social halls directed more to the Chinese community show up there and on the side streets.

More than sixty restaurants offer many styles of cuisine. These include specialties in *dim sum* (a selection of dishes from carts or trays), the everyday *wo choy,* even noodles. Both markets and restaurants present visual tantalizations and rich aromas.

The monumental Chinese cultural center in the Holiday Inn, 750 Kearny, is a focal point for exhibits and tours, reached by a footbridge over Kearny from Portsmouth Square — itself a Chinatown landmark. This park, also underlaid by a parking structure, is where American sovereignty was proclaimed in 1846, and it has many associations with Robert Louis Stevenson. Today it is a social gathering place for Chinese — one surpassed in popularity only by the Friday-to-Sunday outdoor food market nearby on Stockton for three blocks south from Broadway.

WEST, EAST, AND NORTH OF CHINATOWN

Three personality areas cluster around three sides of Chinatown. They form colorful parts of the city mosaic, though all are not necessarily goals for the pedestrian.

The first one is for walkers, though: Nob Hill, west up the California Street slope by cable car. Here are two landmarks from when the nineteenth-century silver and railroad barons lived here: Huntington Park marks the site of the C. P. Huntington mansion, and the still-standing Flood mansion houses the reticent Pacific Union Club. Sharing the heights are Grace Cathedral (Episcopalian) and three of the city's most famous hostelries: the Mark Hopkins, the Fairmont, and the Stanford Court.

Then east of Chinatown is the four-block area known loosely as Jackson Square: Montgomery to Battery and Washington to Pacific. In a nostalgic setting, its restored warehouses, stables, banks, and other Old San Francisco commercial buildings mostly house suppliers and designers in the fields of architecture and interiors. Once along the waterfront (before the days of massive landfill), the area includes the infamous Barbary Coast.

To the north of Chinatown is a larger but more diffuse area, North Beach, also along the water before landfill. Today it is the Italian community, expressed in groceries, restaurants, bakeries and other shops, and liberally sprinkled with small crafts places.

The main axis of North Beach is the great diagonal of Columbus Avenue, which cuts off a corner of the park at the heart of the district — Washington Square, fronted by the church of Sts. Peter and Paul. The major intersecting street, toward the southeast end, is considerably less spiritual: Broadway, the city's most publicized night-spot location.

THE NORTH WATERFRONT

Columbus Avenue points northwest like an arrow to the north waterfront, the most extraordinary concentration of visitor attractions in Western America.

You can get there the fun way on the cable car from downtown. Take either the Powell, Hyde and Beach, or the Powell, Bay and Taylor; both have turnarounds at the waterfront — the former in pretty little Victorian Park. Otherwise, come early if you want a parking place.

The district is slightly larger than Chinatown. It extends about from Pier 43 west past Fisherman's Wharf to Aquatic Park and from Bay Street north to the bay shore.

Its marine resources are unusually varied. One is simply the fishing fleet parked in view of restaurants and seafood markets on Fisherman's Wharf and surrounds. There are bay cruises ($1\frac{1}{4}$ hours) and Alcatraz Island trips (reservations: 546-2805) near the Wharf. Seven ships are on display: the windjammer *Balclutha,* a replica of Sir Francis Drake's *Golden Hinde,* and five veterans — including a bay ferry — at San Francisco Maritime State Historic Park. And the streamlined Maritime Museum is the anchor for Aquatic Park.

Onshore is a thriving and usually thronged array of shops and shopping complexes. Notable among them are two big revivals: The Cannery, of which the name reflects the former use, and Ghirardelli Square, a more diverse group of ex-chocolate factory and ancillary buildings. All are tastefully landscaped and graphically unassailable.

There are also some purely tourist enterprises. And some unusual ones. One place, the Wine Museum, at Beach and Hyde, is especially worth a visit. Another, the Buena Vista Cafe is a real landmark, the revered (if visually unimpressive) shrine to Irish Coffee.

THE GOLDEN GATE PROMENADE

This shoreline segment of the city is remarkable for its wild, open shore — where you walk eye-to-eye with great ships going by — much of it visible only by pedestrians.

It is part of the Golden Gate National Recreation Area, an immense shoreline strip park on both sides of the Golden Gate. The walk extends from Fort Mason, beside Aquatic Park, west three miles to Fort Point. Events along the way are beaches and seawalls, clumps of trees and open greenswards, rowing and swimming clubs and bocce ball courts, boat moorages and piers.

If the whole length seems too much to walk, you can start at such intermediate points as the Marina and Palace of Fine Arts parks. The latter holds the stately open-dome pavilion designed by Bernard Maybeck for the 1915 exposition. A temporary structure when built, it was recreated in permanent form in 1967. Today it houses the Exploratorium, a kind of hands-on set of science-technology displays — some of them good fun indeed.

To the west you enter wilder country, largely unbuilt upon because it was part of the huge Presidio Army reservation. Again you pass beach and rocky shore, and such landmarks as Crissy Field — from which the China Clipper pioneered Pacific airline flights in the 1930's — a Coast Guard station, and the former Mine Dock.

The climax is the point, with its Civil War Fort Winfield Scott, placed here to guard the harbor entrance at its narrowest point. The narrowness accounts also for the presence of the Golden Gate Bridge here, soaring high above. For years the fort was lost to view under the southern arch of the bridge. Now it is restored and open as a museum.

THE 49-MILE DRIVE

Visitors are usually advised to start with the 49-Mile Drive, a sign-posted scenic route for motorists, as an aid to orientation. I have saved it for now because I think it is more worthwhile to experience the vital northeast corner of the city as a set of first impressions.

The exploration so far has taken us through an angular crescent from downtown northeast on Market, northwest on Columbus, and west along the shore of the bay. The 49-Mile Drive traverses this swath and much more. It's not so well marked that you don't need a map — and probably a navigator — though. Some turns are easy to miss. Among several sources for the map is the San Francisco Convention and Visitors Bureau, 1390 Market Street, San Francisco 94102.

The route totals closer to seventy than to forty-nine miles. That latter number is popularly held to refer to the Gold Rush year — so critical in the city's development, rather than to actual mileage.

I wouldn't follow the whole tour, though it's fine if you have lots of time and like to drive. Even the shorter route I suggest can take from several hours to all day, depending on the stops you make. The scenic best of San Francisco lies north of a line through Golden Gate Park, Twin Peaks, and Market street — the segment of the drive described here.

Starting from the Golden Gateway area, the route takes you west on Washington, south on Battery, then west and up the steepness of California Street through Chinatown and across Nob Hill. At Gough you turn left (south).

Then at Geary, a main thoroughfare, turn west and in a few blocks you will come to the parking garage entrance for Japan Town, a five-acre complex of hotel, shops, eating and refreshment places, and a festival site. It's an Oriental enclave in modern trappings, including a striking pagoda.

Back on Gough, turn south, then at Grove turn east for a look at the monumental Civic Center. The marked route turns north on Van Ness, passing through one end of the Civic Center, though it shows you the two buildings of most importance to the visitor: the opera house and the Veterans Building, which houses the San Francisco Museum of Art.

Still, I suggest a loop through the center to glimpse some of the extent of this remarkable assemblage of Beaux Arts structures. Continue east on Grove, then go north on Larkin and turn west on McAllister to Van Ness — where you continue the drive north. This takes you along the great plaza and past the facade of City Hall intended to be the most impressive.

Then after another downtown transit you go out past (and up) Telegraph Hill, the north waterfront district, the Marina, the Presidio, and Lincoln Park. Here the centerpiece is another Beaux Arts structure with the rather lofty name of California Palace of the Legion of Honor. It is a museum of old master paintings, graphic and other works, and a sculpture collection rich in Rodin pieces — including one of the three casts of *The Thinker* in California.

Moving west again on Geary, you reach the coast at Cliff House, opposite Seal Rocks and overlooking the long straight stretch of beach to the south — down beside which the route then drops.

Soon you are opposite Golden Gate Park. It is here that I advise turning inland.

Take any of the easterly park roads (see the next section, below). They lead to Stanyan Street at the east end of the main part of the park, where you turn south to resume the scenic drive. Follow it to Twin Peaks, one of the city's premier vista points. Then stay on it down and onto Market Street — off which there is one recommended detour. The goal of this side trip is the mission; go east on Sixteenth Street to Dolores Street, where you will see it. Then go north on Dolores to Market and stay on it until you reach downtown.

GOLDEN GATE PARK

Like Balboa Park in San Diego, Golden Gate Park is one of America's great parks.

About the same size as Balboa Park (more than 1,100 acres), it cuts an impressive rectangular green slice out of paved and built-up city. And it gets even more use than Balboa, perhaps, because though San Francisco is smaller in population than San Diego, its area is considerably smaller. Thus it is far more densely settled, providing the classic constituency for park space and services.

Like Balboa Park, Golden Gate Park is a center for some heavily-used urban (even non-park) functions. Here are two major museums. One, "the De Young," is the city's most active art museum. The other, the lively California Academy of Sciences, has an aquarium and a planetarium besides its animal and other natural-history exhibits.

Nearby are some more typically park-oriented facilities: a Japanese tea garden, a music concourse with seats under pollarded plane trees, an arboretum with a hall of flowers, and east of the center of activity an utterly charming Victorian conservatory.

For the rest, the park is devoted to the outdoors, including the linear pursuits of bicycling, walking, and jogging. It is three and a half miles (excluding the eastern extension, the "Panhandle") of forest and lawn, of rhododendrons and tree ferns that flourish in a climate that also favors redwood forest, of glades and meadows — one of them with a bison herd — and nearly a dozen lakes and ponds.

And there are arenas, courts, and courses, too, to accommodate sports familiar and exotic, along with two stadiums and specialized facilities for model yachting, fly-casting, lawn bowls, dog training, and equitation — among others.

THE VIEW

It all tends to come together when seen from above. If you are in the city on a sparkling clear day or a day of dramatic fog banks or a clear night, you can seek out four extraordinary overlook sites in this town famous for its views. The first two are also on the 49-Mile Drive, but you can use these directions to get there from the downtown area.

Twin Peaks presents the most extensive panorama from the highest elevation. You look from the sea to the bay and beyond, over the city. To get there, take Market Street southwest to well beyond its straight section, where it becomes Portola Drive, then angle back to the right on Twin Peaks Boulevard.

Telegraph Hill is an in-town eminence from which you get a more intimate view, particularly over the waterfront immediately below. From Columbus Avenue, take Lombard east. It leads to the top, which is capped by the stiff landmark of Coit Tower.

Yerba Buena Island presents the classic look at the city skyline rising above the bay-side waterfront, with the curves of the bridge cables in the foreground. Take the Bay Bridge halfway across, then the Treasure Island exit.

And Fort Baker affords several locations on the Marin County side of the Golden Gate for dramatic views of the city. Take the Golden Gate Bridge and exit just beyond it.

And lastly there are four nighttime eyries for contemplating the city lightscape. The Fairmont's Crown Room and the Top of the Mark, across the street, have the highest altitude. The Carnelian Room atop the Bank of America building downtown surveys the supertower scene. And the revolving Equinox Room of the Hyatt Regency offers its own spectacular vista over waterfront and bay.

Imperial Mammoth sculpture in tar-seep lake, Hancock Park

Chapter 3:

Los Angeles

LOS ANGELES GETS its ranking here not because two other cities are greater, but because they are smaller and structured so as to be slightly easier for the vacationer to experience. You have to work a little harder to get at the best of Los Angeles, but the effort is worthwhile in the sense of discovery it yields.

The metropolis is spread out, so here is a plan of attack that assumes a base of operations in the downtown center — once more the visitor magnet it was long ago, with new hotels and highrise towers built in recent years.

You can stay at one of five big first-class hotels downtown, or in one of a sprinkling of smaller but still comfortable places. For a list of accommodations, along with maps and other information, write to Greater Los Angeles Visitors and Convention Bureau, 505 South Flower Street, Los Angeles 90071 or telephone (213) 488-9100 (or on weekdays drop in at their office underground in Arco Plaza.)

I assume that once established you will be prepared to drive around, as residents do. Though seldom noted, most of the great-city features of Los Angeles occupy a compact swath of territory in the form of a double arc — like the head-on silhouette of a seagull. Thus the vastness of what the city map shows is not something you need worry about conquering.

One arc reaches from downtown northeast through the Arroyo Seco (the canyon through which the Pasadena Freeway runs) then east through Pasadena, San Marino, and Arcadia. The other arc, a little longer, stretches from downtown northwest, then west and southwest along the foot of the Santa Monica Mountains to the sea. The first arc extends into the San Gabriel Valley; the second is on the uppermost reach of the vast, flat Los Angeles Plain.

EXPLORING DOWNTOWN

The downtown district comes in two parts: the commercial section and the prominent Civic Center — which contains city, county, state, and federal buildings and the Music Center.

The commercial section is small, as major-city downtowns go: only about eight blocks (though long ones, to be sure) in a north-south direction, and five to six much shorter blocks east-west.

One result of this is that you can see highlights on foot. For a tour, start at centrally-located Pershing Square, atop underground parking. In the following itinerary, note that many places are closed on Sundays:

Go north on Hill, then just south of Third, cross through the vast food bazaar of the Grand Central Public Market to Broadway. On the corner just to the north, notice the elaborate facade of Sid Grauman's 1918 Million Dollar Theatre, and across from it go inside the magic Bradbury Building — all nineteenth-century cast-iron ornament and light and soaring, balconied spaces.

Go south along Broadway — lively with signs and voices in Spanish and the sounds of Latin music and the aromas of Mexican food — to Seventh. Half a block west, between Bullock's department store buildings, look in on St. Vincent's Alley, with its outdoor espresso bar and sidewalk florist.

West on Seventh, the Broadway Plaza occupies the block between Hope and Flower — first of seven superblocks on our route and site of a major hotel, department store (the first new one downtown in years), shops, and restaurants around a skylit mall.

North on Flower, new axis of the financial community, go underground at Sixth through Arco Plaza's two levels of shops and eating places — underneath two gargantuan black glass office towers.

Then an escalator and a pedestrian bridge — one of a half dozen downtown — lift you across Fifth into the stack of mirrored cylinders that is the Bonaventure Hotel, opened in 1977. From its sixth-level outdoor garden another bridge takes you across Figueroa to a de facto park: Union Bank Plaza. And from the eighth level inside, beyond the huge six-story circular lobby, still another bridge crosses high above Fourth into the two-story mall of the World Trade Center — with its shops, showrooms, and the U.S. Passport Office.

A fourth bridge crosses Flower to the fortress-like podium from which sprouts the immense tower of Security Pacific Plaza. You enter on the concourse level, with shops, a garden open to the sky, and restaurants (closed weekends) open to the garden. Go to the upper level (atop Bunker Hill, the city's redevelopment area) to see the tall, airy lobby where art exhibits are often shown, and look outside at the towering red steel Calder sculpture in a plaza beside a garden like a public park, covering a city block.

South of that, another rooftop garden crowns the Arco parking structure, and down on Fifth beyond that is the city's Main Library — its grounds like a small park. Its tower, capped with a polychrome tile pyramid, encloses a high second-story rotunda, grand in scale, from the old days of intense civic pride.

Then just to the east you can walk through the Biltmore Hotel, restored in 1977 to its opulent glory of half a century earlier, through its paneled corridors, past sumptuous public rooms, and down into the lofty Renaissance lobby facing Olive Street — where you came out on Pershing Square, start of the walk.

CIVIC CENTER AND THE ETHNIC DISTRICTS

For this exploration, probably the best place to start is near City Hall — its unmistakable landmark tower once the tallest building in town. There is parking under the two-block-long Los Angeles Mall, out of which rises City Hall East. You can walk the Mall's embowered promenades — surface and below ground — and browse the shops of this combination park and mini-shopping center on city premises.

A covered pedestrian bridge crosses from City Hall East over to the main City Hall, where elevators take you up to the tower (open office hours, weekdays; afternoons, weekends) for a wide view over the plain and the city immediately below.

From City Hall you can hike up the hill to the plaza and three theaters of the Music Center, commandingly sited at the upper end of the Civic Center. You walk partly through the landscaped County Mall, which stretches for several blocks between Temple and First Streets.

And from City Hall you can walk a short distance east on First into Little Tokyo, cultural and commercial center for Los Angeles' extensive Japanese-descent community. Highlights are the 1977 New Otani Hotel, with its roof garden, and shops, restaurants, and Buddhist temples on First and Second Streets.

Then north of the Los Angeles Mall, you cross the freeway to the old Plaza, where Los Angeles began. Around the Plaza are restorations of the city's first firehouse and Pico House hotel, Merced Theatre, and Masonic Hall. The old plaza church has been in use continually since the 1820's.

And Olvera Street, the city's renowned pedestrian way, lined with stalls, shops, and restaurants and offering the merchandise and foods of Mexico, opens off the Plaza. Though well known and often crowded, it is more than a mere tourist trap. Paper piñatas and paper flowers, a red old-fashioned popcorn wagon, a tropical fruit stand, and strolling musicians add life and color.

East across Alameda from the Plaza rises the stately Union Passenger Terminal, a monument from 1939 and the days when this was the entry point for most visitors to Los Angeles. Quiet now, though a few Amtrak trains come and go, it is nonetheless worth the short walk to see its grand halls, colorful stonework, and Art Deco bronze.

Then proceeding northerly, you pass through several blocks of gradually increasing evidence of the expansion of the Chinese community in the last few years. The actual Chinatown extends about four blocks in either direction: Spring to Hill, and Ord to New Chinatown — the pedestrian mall complex of shops and restaurants built forty years ago when the Union Station displaced a former Chinatown.

EASTERN ARC: *San Gabriel Valley*

The civilized arts — landscape, architecture, painting, sculpture, literature — infuse this foray east from downtown. And you see nine old houses, from a humble adobe cottage to one of America's great houses, on display and displaying treasures and memorabilia. I will start with the farthest site and work back:

In Arcadia, the Los Angeles State and County Arboretum is a huge parklike garden of often colorful exotic plants. You also see relics of former owners Hugo Reid (his adobe house) and "Lucky" Baldwin (a gem of a Queen Anne cottage), a reconstruction of the rail station Baldwin made Santa Fe build as a condition for crossing his estate, a small lake, a jungle that has been used in films.

Not far west in San Marino, Henry E. Huntington's former estate — the Huntington Library, Art Gallery and Botanical Garden — is a goal for travelers from the world over. The grounds display rare plants, a Japanese garden, and other specialty gardens. The library's six million items include a Gutenberg Bible, the Ellesmere Chaucer, Benjamin Franklin's hand-written autobiography, and other rarities on exhibit. The art gallery displays the largest study collection of eighteenth-century British painting outside London and a remarkable array of decorative arts.

Then with a little study of a street map, you can plot a route west through Pasadena, past the campus of Cal Tech, past the Chinese-style Pacificulture-Asia Museum, past Pasadena's 1920's neo-baroque Civic Center, and on to the Norton Simon Museum at Colorado and Orange Grove (an intersection made famous by the Rose Parade). Another world-stature collection, it has paintings from many periods and grounds that constitute one of the city's three most distinguished sculpture gardens.

Also worth a look, though open only a couple of days a week, are two estates on Orange Grove not far north of the museum.

One is the Pasadena Historical Society, at the corner of Walnut, in an old mansion in a four-acre forested garden. Exhibits take you back via early photography and artifacts to early Pasadena, and the mansion's rooms are still opulently furnished from their early twentieth-century heyday.

Diagonally across Orange Grove, on Westmoreland Place, you can see the exquisite 1908 Gamble House, an imposing two-story shingled masterpiece by Charles and Henry Greene, celebrated architects of the Craftsman era. The interior, worth coming back to see on a tour day, was completely designed by the Greenes: stained glass, carpets, furniture, even light fixtures.

Then head south on Orange Grove to get to the Pasadena Freeway, the return route to downtown. At the corner of Arbor, note the ornate Wrigley mansion, once the western home of the chewing-gum tycoon, now headquarters of the Tournament of Roses organization.

On the return, allow time for a side trip off the Pasadena Freeway: Exit at Avenue 43 and you will be near three monuments of the past, all clearly visible. Heritage Square, a refuge for threatened old buildings, contains the handsome Hale House restoration and others in progress. The nearby Charles Lummis House was hand-crafted by one of the city's most colorful early characters. And up on the hill above, the Southwest Museum — of which Lummis was a principal founder — was a pioneer in the study of the Indians of America.

WESTERN ARC: *Out Wilshire, Back Sunset*

Still the prestige address, Wilshire Boulevard, is the site of hotels, corporate-ego-gratifying office buildings, showcase churches, and top-of-the-market stores — the prototypical strip development sanctified by monetary success. The visitor notes a running catalog of the non-residential Good Life of Southern California, in which the interest concentrates at three points: Hancock Park, Beverly Hills, and Westwood.

Hancock Park first achieved fame as the site of the "tar pits" of Rancho La Brea, seeps of asphaltum over which water spread, so that animals of the Pleistocene age that came to drink were entrapped — and their bones perfectly preserved. One of the lakes persists, decorated today by life-size reproductions of sabre-toothed cat and imperial mammoth. Nearby, the Page Museum graphically presents the story and displays the skeletons, and in other parts of the park you can descend into an observation pit and observe a dig — and look over the shoulders of paleontologists studying current finds.

The park is also the site of the three-pavilioned Los Angeles County Museum of Art. A cultural focal point for the community, it is adorned outside with impressive Rodin and contemporary pieces in a two-part sculpture garden. At this writing, the museum's holdings had outgrown its space and it was planning expansion into buildings across from the park.

While in the neighborhood, don't miss the smaller Craft and Folk Art Museum, across Wilshire and slightly to the east. It is also a shop, a restaurant, and a theater and school for members.

Beverly Hills is one of the small satellite downtowns that give flavor to the metropolis. And the super-prestige address. Here the big department stores — Saks, Robinson's, Neiman-Marcus, I. Magnin, Bonwit Teller — front on Wilshire, as does the elegant Beverly Wilshire Hotel. It is worth a stroll about, with an obligatory side trip up Rodeo Drive and back past the classy boutiques and branches of New York and European stores. Even window shopping, it's an excursion into the wonderful madness of the upper edge of the consumer scale.

To see another mini-downtown, take a side trip on Santa Monica Boulevard a short distance southwest to the highrise private-enterprise development of Century City (its name comes from its origin as the Twentieth Century-Fox studio backlot). Here are arrayed office buildings, vertical residential structures, a shopping center, a major hotel (the Century Plaza), and the ABC Entertainment Center — with restaurants, a legitimate theater (the Shubert), and two movie houses all in one complex.

Farther out Wilshire, Westwood is still another mini-downtown, with its charming village-scale shops from the 1920's — many of them unfortunately much remodeled — and its later-generation larger buildings, up to highrise towers. Its neighbor to the north — UCLA — put Westwood on the map when it was a struggling real estate development out in the country. Today, it is a pleasant place for pedestrians and it contains perhaps the city's greatest concentration of movie theaters — a good many of them first-run houses.

Continue out Wilshire through Santa Monica to where the boulevard ends at Palisades Park — a great place for a stop and a stroll under the palms along the bluff-top overlooking the beach and the sea, with perhaps a side trip down to the funky old Santa Monica Pier.

Then go north a block from Wilshire and take the California Ramp down to the coast highway — headed northwest, then west — or upcoast. Bring your bathing suit if it's beach weather (and if you can find a parking place; here is where Angelenos come flocking, and on good days it's full by eleven in the morning). Santa Monica State Beach along here is a series of parking lots — gaps between houses where properties have come into State ownership and have been opened for public access. To seaward is one of the broadest sand beaches on the coast.

Then at the Santa Monica-Los Angeles boundary you come to Will Rogers State Beach, more open and once the humorist's private domain.

The goal now is the J. Paul Getty Museum, about a mile beyond the end of Sunset Boulevard. A reproduction in living color of a Roman great house, it is set in a garden of plants from the Mediterranean (the climate is almost the same here), and it houses excellent Greek and Roman antiquities, European painting, and decorative arts. Alas, Roman villas, even in Southern California, don't have much parking space, so you need a parking reservation; call ahead for one at 454-6541.

Then backtrack along the coast highway and turn inland on Sunset Boulevard for a drive through the residential Good Life of Southern California. Some notable sights along the way:

☐ The charming little lake and garden of the Self-Realization Fellowship, with its bo tree, its Indian lotus temple, and ashes of Mahatma Gandi.

☐ The 1920's ranch of Will Rogers, complete with polo field — now a State Historic Park and gateway to the trails of the great wild Topanga State Park in the Santa Monicas beyond.

☐ The campus of UCLA, beyond the San Diego Freeway. You can walk grounds as handsomely planted as gardens. Particularly noteworthy is the sculpture garden in the north campus area, fronting the Wight Gallery — frequent locale of art exhibits. There is a parking structure close by, free on Sundays, near the Sunset-Hilgard corner of the campus.

☐ The affluent suburbs of Bel Air and Beverly Hills, alternating ostentation with an urge to privacy in the form of fifteen-foot-high hedges.

☐ The mildly outrageous commercialism of the Sunset Strip, a real Hollywood flash setting, made jazzy with its handpainted super-billboards trumpeting the glories of the day in the entertainment industry.

☐ The somewhat ordinary Hollywood section, in which such landmarks as the Palladium and the Cinerama dome benefit from the charitable mantle of night.

From Hollywood east, Sunset gets increasingly funkier as you get into older suburbs in toward the center of town — from the 1920's, even the 1880's. I enjoy this section for its residential scale and its evocation of the past; some people do not.

For an alternate route, go up (north) to Hollywood Boulevard on La Brea and turn east to see the tourist center. Its landmarks are: on the west, the exuberant Grauman's (now Mann's) Chinese Theatre, and on the east, the circular Capitol Records tower and the Pantages — now a legitimate theater. In between are a concentrated bookstore district of surprising variety, tourist shops, enough theaters to make this a major movie district, and the raunchy nighttime street action so much in the headlines in recent years.

Beyond, Hollywood Boulevard goes through another aging area while pursuing the goal of Barnsdall Park, just west of Vermont Avenue. Here is Frank Lloyd Wright's famous Hollyhock House, now restored and open to the public on occasion, and the Municipal Art Gallery, scene of some interesting shows. All are on the eminence of Olive Hill (named for the trees that clothe its sides), once the estate of Aline Barnsdall, who donated it to the city for an art center.

At Vermont turn left (north) and go up into Griffith Park, past the Greek Theatre and the Bird Sanctuary to the Observatory. This contains a planetarium, science hall, and telescopes, and its parapets offer one of the most spreading views of Los Angeles to be seen anywhere — a suitable climax to a visit on a sparkling clear day (most likely in fall and winter). For the return, downtown is close in view.

The foregoing sketches a sampling only of visitable chunks of the city. There are of course other places: Exposition Park, with its museums; the Coliseum, Sports Arena, Forum, Pauley Pavilion, Dodger and Anaheim stadiums, and the racetracks for sporting events; the Hollywood Bowl; Universal Studios (best way to glimpse the film thing); the Orange County amusement parks (Chapter 9); the two harbors (Chapter 12), miles of beaches, miles of mountains, and other places to go. Happy exploring; the city can seem endless.

Low tide uncovers rocky pools below cliffs in Pacific Grove

Chapter 4:

Monterey Peninsula

THE PENINSULA seems to generate excitement every time I see it on the approach across the artichoke fields that mark the final flat spread of the Salinas Valley. It is as if some magical presence lurked there ahead, investing its wooded heights, its foam-flecked rocky shores, intense white sand beaches, and the haven where the explorers dropped anchor with portentous meaning.

This four by five-mile rectangular projection of land into the Pacific, forming the southern end of Monterey Bay, has more of a sense of place than most places I have seen.

History may partly account for this. It focused on the town of Monterey, long somnolent as an outpost of Spanish empire, then slightly more active as the Mexican capital of Alta California, then prominent in the American conquest, and finally again quiet as a fishing port while a resort grew nearby for the American East and for San Francisco.

The sense of place is undoubtedly enhanced by the peninsula's role in literature, as described by Richard Henry Dana (" . . . the pleasantest and most civilized-looking place in California") and Robert Louis Stevenson and Robinson Jeffers and John Steinbeck — about as diverse a set of observers as one can imagine. It's bound to color anyone's view, for there is more than a little déjà vu when you finally step into a scene about which you have read vivid description.

Certainly some of the individuality comes from the magnetism of a landscape that has a distinct personality, unique with native pines and cypress that are among the oldest kinds of plants on earth and relics of a climatic era that has hardly changed in millenia. Or sea animals that survive from ages ago or that have come back — as the sea otter has — from the brink of extinction within decades.

Or maybe the effect is just hyper-atmospheric, with old Monterey and Puritan Pacific Grove and escapist Carmel all tinged, in Stevenson's words, by " . . . the haunting presence of the ocean . . . The woods and the Pacific rule between them the climate — when the air does not smell salt from the one it will be blowing perfumed from the resinous tree tops of the other."

Whatever the diagnosis, the magnetism is undeniable, and the place has to rank high as one of California's jewels.

MONTEREY, *City With a Past*

As in most port towns, the waterfront commands attention and is the easiest landmark for the motorist to find, so you may as well park here — the parking lot is the biggest in town — and get this part of your visit out of the way first.

It's all rather colorful, even the Municipal Wharf on the east, hangout of pier fishermen and home of commercial fish packers. In between this and the other pier are moored the pleasure craft of the Marina. The more western pier is the tourist-oriented Fisherman's Wharf — a place often lively as crowds throng its seafood markets (try a crab cocktail to go), eateries, souvenir shops, and other enterprises. Here is where you catch a fishing party boat, and here is where the organ grinder and his monkey entertain on a weekend afternoon.

Facing the waterfront is one of the most charming historical buildings in California, the Mexican-period Custom House. Oldest government building on the coast (circa 1827), it is one of the prime adornments of Monterey State Historic Park. This virtually boundary-less entity is made up of nine buildings and their premises, along with the site where Navigator Sebastián Vizcaíno landed in 1602 (Pacific, just south of Artillery Street). The same site was found later by Captain Gaspar de Portolá and Father Junípero Serra when on June 3, 1770 they formally founded Monterey.

The pieces of the park — like other parts of Old Monterey — come in two clusters. One is near the waterfront and one is south and inland, in the vicinity of City Hall.

You get plenty of help in seeing the antiquities. The park's own brochure contains a map, along with portraits and descriptions of the buildings. Then you can pick up a downtown walking tour map published by the Old Monterey Council for a more detailed inventory of private as well as public buildings. And the Monterey Path of History — a driving tour past some forty-five old places — is also presented as a map. You can pick up a copy (along with lists of places to stay, restaurants, points of interest, and golf courses) at the chamber of commerce in the Monterey Fairgrounds Travelodge at 2030 Fremont Street.

I won't try to duplicate the literature with a description of each site, but here are some notes on where to look on a history walk through town. (Note that most of the state park places close from noon to 1 P.M.).

Besides the Custom House (outfitted as a museum) the seaward cluster contains the big 1847 Pacific House, across a pleasant open pedestrian plaza. Restored and perhaps the grandest of the Monterey-style adobes — characteristically two stories with a balcony — it is also a museum that features Monterey and Indian lore. Behind is a Memory Garden — one of a dozen charming old-time gardens in town — through which you can walk on the way to the 1850's Boston Store restoration — also called "Casa del Oro."

Then if you have plenty of time you can walk north on Olivier Street and turn left for a block past the city's first brick house (as opposed to the far more common sun-dried adobe) and the whaling station — both for outside-only looking — and return south on Pacific a block to the first theater in California. Or, go directly west from the Boston Store on Scott to the theater.

Like most memorable old Monterey establishments, this one can be seen from afar by virtue of its landmark Monterey cypress tree (they all must have been planted before anyone realized how huge they can grow in cultivation). Inside, the 1846-47 building is interesting to tour, but the best way to experience it is when a performance is actually taking place; the usual fare is nineteenth-century plays.

Then the Old Church (a library), the Doud House, and the Perry House — all a block west via Scott on Van Buren Street — complete the seaward historical group.

From there I would simply walk back to Pacific and turn south (inland), for it is then just three blocks to the other cluster of interest — past the Soberanes and Merritt houses and Capitular Hall, all private.

Or, if you want to conserve your strength, move your car to the downtown vicinity. There is parking off Pacific and Calle Principal, south of Franklin Street.

The inland district is bounded by Jefferson and Pearl streets on the north and Madison, Hartnell, and Webster on the south. And it runs from Dutra on the west to Houston on the east.

One of the most fascinating old districts in California, it has a jumbled street pattern that may be the despair of traffic engineers (and motorists), but this makes for charm to enchant the stroller — along with walk-through garden spaces between streets and small parks on left-over land. The street layout reflects the random placement of the earliest adobes, when "streets" were afterthought spaces between buildings.

The state park has five buildings or building groups in this section, of which the most important is undoubtedly the well-furnished Larkin House from the 1830's, at Jefferson and Calle Principal. It was the home of the influential United States Consul in the years immediately preceding the American conquest of California.

Also notable are the 1841 Gutiérrez House (Calle Principal just north of Madison), in use as a restaurant; the "Stevenson House" (Houston between Pearl and Webster) — actually the González-Girardin House, where the writer stayed in 1879; and the Cooper-Molera Adobe (Polk at Munras), which is being restored. A fifth, Soberanes, is not yet open.

Other structures are in public ownership other than State or open under other auspices: Colton Hall, the splendid two-story town hall (beside City Hall) where the drafting of the California constitution took place, the old jail nearby, the maritime and art museums, the Amesti House. Still others are in private use, though usually marked, or private but open in such functions as Gallatin's Restaurant in the Stokes Adobe.

If you have made this a walking tour all the way, you can return seaward on Alvarado Street past two more adobes — Sánchez and Rodríguez. You will also pass the handsome new Monterey Conference Center — a complex of pedestrian spaces, meeting halls, theater, and hotel that replaces several seedy blocks between downtown and the waterfront.

Other historic places are passed on the driving tour. At least one of them — the Royal Chapel, on two-block-long Church Street — is worth a stop. Dating from 1794 and in use since then, it resembles the mission at Carmel (having been done by the same designer at the same time), though executed in more sophisticated lines. It is the only presidio chapel left in California.

Then east of the town center are the greenbelts, landscaped areas around the remnants of former estuaries. One of these is pleasant El Estero Park on Del Monte Avenue, favored of waterfowl and small children — for whom special play equipment was designed at the Dennis the Menace Playground.

The other is the campus of the Naval Postgraduate School, reached from a main entrance at Sloat and Third. The school is the successor to the Del Monte Hotel, parent of Del Monte Lodge in Pebble Beach (see "Seventeen-Mile Drive" below). Vintage 1880, the hotel buildings were replaced after a fire in 1924, and the school has occupied those buildings and the grounds since 1951. You can drive through the parklike surroundings on a circular road, passing small Del Monte Lake. The nearby Old Del Monte Golf Course, another relic of the former hotel, is said to have been the first course west of the Mississippi.

Monterey's other focus of interest is northwest of the town center, beyond the gap of the Presidio army reservation: Cannery Row.

Of it, Steinbeck has written much, including this note on the ecological disaster that ended its first career, in 1954: "Cannery Row was sad when all the pilchards [sardines] were caught and canned and eaten. The pearl-gray canneries of corrugated iron were silent . . . The street that once roared with trucks was quiet and empty."

But after a few years the Steinbeck charisma took hold and the funky charm of cavernous empty buildings — available at low rent — became apparent. A few shops and restaurants opened, and before long a nearly eight-block stretch of erstwhile factories exploded into a kind of branch San Francisco Fisherman's Wharf rendered in gray — and lively by day and night. Even now that it has been thoroughly discovered, it is often good fun.

PACIFIC GROVE

Adjoining Monterey on the northwest, this town provides a link between the developed shore and the wild. It's mainly a residential community, with some excellent Victorian survivors, a nice little natural history museum, and an unexpected trove of near-shore places to stay — plus, of course, a million migrating Monarch butterflies that swarm in well-marked trees every October.

I especially like the long clifftop shoreline drive of Ocean View Boulevard. It evokes La Jolla and Sunset Cliffs in San Diego and is equally as picturesque, with surf alternating with vast tidepools on a wild, rocky shore. It presents a sort of toll-free preview of the Seventeen-Mile Drive beyond, though more citified on its inward side. The shore features include Lovers Point, a modern contraction from the "Lovers of Jesus Point" of the old days when the town was still the Methodist retreat for which is was founded.

One gem stands out, the old Pt. Pinos Lighthouse, as romantic in form and site as they come. A contemporary and virtually a twin of the light on Point Loma in San Diego, it got into service earlier in the year of 1855, and therefore is "older." You can visit it on weekend afternoons. The point was named for the peninsula's native Monterey pines — impressive to early navigators up from the treeless coast to the south.

Pacific Grove's westernmost reach is not Pt. Pinos, but Asilomar State Beach and Conference Grounds. This is just the group facility its name implies, though individuals can stay here if there are unoccupied rooms. It's a retreat of dunes, surf, cypress — and often fog — with a genuine sense of remoteness. The property forms the boundary between the city and the private Del Monte Properties enclave — nearly two-thirds of the peninsula — to the south, reached via the slow but spectacular course of the Seventeen-Mile Drive.

SEVENTEEN-MILE DRIVE

This famous road, which clings to the shore of nearly half the peninsula, is not seventeen miles long. It takes its name from the length of an old-time outing loop route from the original Del Monte Hotel over in Monterey.

With few if any rivals in California among scenic roads, the drive is worth the cost ($4 at this writing) at least once. And it is eased by an excellent map you get at the toll gate.

The seaside section detailed here, from the Pacific Grove gate to the Carmel gate, is about nine miles long. Crashing surf is the dominant element much of the time. The drive takes you close to it, past dune-lined beach and picturesque rocky cliff (and an occasional house), past the turbulent waters of Point Joe and along seas smoothed by kelp beds, past native Monterey pines and cypress — including the Lone Cypress, the single most-often-pictured tree in California.

Offshore rocks are named for bird and seals (gulls and cormorants, sea lions and harbor seals), which you will see. On shore, you may glimpse deer, relaxed in the knowledge of their safety from the hunter's bullet.

You drive past five golf courses, several of them of world renown, including the Spyglass Hill, Cypress Point, and Pebble Beach courses, rated — respectively — among the top forty, twenty, and ten in America.

There are designated picnic areas along the way, or you can stop for lunch at the elegant former Del Monte Lodge, now The Lodge at Pebble Beach (see Chapter 11), overlooking the eighteenth hole of the Pebble Beach Golf Links. (The Lodge was started in 1919 as a kind of woodsy outpost of the Del Monte Hotel.)

And then at the Carmel gate, you leave the idyllic barony of Del Monte Forest for an outside world that in its own way is just as woodsy and almost as special.

CARMEL-BY-THE-SEA

Though Carmel may not, strictly speaking, be physically part of the Monterey Peninsula, it is certainly contiguous and psychologically related.

In my estimation, the allure of Carmel is a tribute to the tree — part native and much planted. Its "downtown" — several blocks wide and centered on Ocean Avenue from Junipero Avenue to Monte Verde Street — is an aggregation of nearly 200 shops of no particular esthetic interest by themselves. Yet, nestled in its tree-softened setting, the place achieves a kind of individual and appealing personality that attracts people — and brings them back.

There are other elements to the ambience, to be sure: human scale (there is only one downtown shopping center, and it is not huge), sign control (neon and other lighting hijinks and billboards are prohibited), and other conscious resistance to the trappings of commercial urbanization. Even parking is left at least partly to natural forces (more demand than supply), though there is a garage at the shopping center.

Carmel is at least worth lunch and an hour or two of a morning or afternoon — or more if you're addicted to shopping as a pastime. The shops in general are of moderate or small size, and both permanent and transient ones are amply mapped and listed in the tourist literature. There are plenty of art galleries and plenty of purveyors of the chic and the timeless in clothing, antiques, housewares, imports, crafts, "gifts," and specialties in foods and wines. There are some excellent restaurants and one celebrated tea shop.

Ocean Avenue reaches down to the sea at its foot at Carmel Beach. The beach is set aside as city park and an attractive place for a stroll along the sandy strand down to ebbtide pools at the southern end. The beach crowd is rationed by available parking.

Edging the beach, Scenic Road is just that. It narrows to the south where houses cluster on the headland, passing such intriguing structures as Robinson Jeffers' stone Tor House. And it offers access to the next beach south, Carmel River State Beach, before returning to town as Carmelo Street.

South of the center, Carmel has one stunning historical treasure: Mission San Carlos Borromeo del Río Carmelo. To get there, take Junipero Avenue to the corner of Lasuen Drive (named for the Franciscan father who actually started this church).

Dating from 1793, it is the eighth church in a succession starting with one Father Serra founded (as the second in the Alta California chain) in Monterey. The mission was moved here in 1771, a year after founding. As with most missions, the fathers decided it was better to get the neophytes away from the sometimes unspiritual influence of the soldiers.

Partisans hold this to be the most beautiful mission in California. Built of stone, it is exquisitely detailed and pleasingly restored. In front is a walled garden with a fountain, and next to the church are a cemetery (said to contain 3,000 Indian burials) on one side and a big arcaded quadrangle on the other.

The interior contains the burial place of Father Serra (and fathers Crespi and Lasuén). Rooms beyond the nave display furniture and other eighteenth-century artifacts, Father Serra's own austere cell, and treasures of ornate Spanish baroque work that he brought to California. As historic headquarters for the California mission system, the church has been awarded the unusual rank of basilica.

CARMEL EAST AND SOUTH

Virtually the only direction in which settlement inspired by Carmel could expand was to the east up Carmel Valley. Thus this flat or gently sloped land has become a microcosm of exurban good-life California: a suburbia of spacious-lot houses and landscaped shopping centers interspersed with golf and country clubs and resorts — including John Gardiner's original Tennis Ranch and Quail Lodge (see Chapter 11) — and ranches, artichoke fields and pastures, and rolling hills of grassland, chaparral, and oaks.

It's inland from the coastal fog influence and a delightful place for a drive or a stay. Some special features include a begonia garden display, the unusual Thunderbird Book Shop restaurant in the Valley Hills Shopping Center, horseback riding, and trout and steelhead fishing in the Carmel River.

Then to the south of Carmel is Point Lobos State Reserve — one of the glories of the Pacific Coast.

This is not a recreation park, but a place to experience a rare landscape of such primeval force it inspired Stevenson, Jeffers, the photographer Edward Weston, and others to memorable statements. The edge of its 1,200 acres is six miles of deeply-indented rocky cliff shore, seething surf, teeming tidepools, and an offshore marine reserve of abalone beds, sea caves, and giant kelp forest at the head of a submarine canyon.

The rocks are the haunt of the now-reviving brown pelican and the huge Steller and the merely large California sea lion, and the kelp rafts are playgrounds for the once-rare sea otter. The upland contains one of only two known natural stands of Monterey cypress (the other is at Point Cypress on the Seventeen-Mile Drive) along with only slightly less scarce stands of Monterey pine and Gowen cypress. It gives you a glimpse of what the best of the peninsula a little way to the north must once have been like.

In the interest of preventing trampling, visitors are sometimes limited. On a day when crowds might be expected, call ahead to (408) 624-4909.

JACKS PEAK REGIONAL PARK

And finally, for a refreshing glimpse of some back country, take the road to Salinas, Highway 68, and opposite the airport you will find the entrance to this relatively new picnic and hiking park. The access road takes you in and up several miles through nearly unspoiled pine forest to near the 1,100-foot high point of the mountains that create the peninsula. From there trails lead through woods and open places, and the views out over Monterey Bay, Carmel Valley and Point Lobos are expansive. The park is open every day, 8 A.M. to dusk.

Ebullient county courthouse is the ultimate in Colonial Revival style

Chapter 5:

Santa Barbara

THE SEA HAS a predominant influence on Santa Barbara, the seaside resort. And so has the past. They combine to give the city a fascinating visible recollection of the early seafaring days.

You can see a Chumash Indian ocean-going canoe, for example, in the natural history museum. And you can see a 1976 reproduction of one in the courthouse; it actually navigated out to the Channel Islands, clearly visible offshore, just as the aborigines' canoes did when Cabrillo first came on the scene in 1542.

And you'll encounter models, pictures, and other reminders of the brig *Pilgrim*. It brought writer-seaman Richard Henry Dana in 1836, to give us his famous word portrait of early Santa Barbara.

You can visit the 1854 Trussell-Winchester adobe, in which the beams are timbers from a shipwreck out on Anacapa Island (lumber has always been rare in this land of few forests).

And you can ride the prototype water taxi from the Depression era. The model for a whole fleet, it first served gambling ships off Los Angeles, then later was a small ferry at Coronado. A sleek, teak craft now named *Shirley-Ann*, it was graduated to more respectable duty here taking visitors on offshore cruise excursions.

The sea and the beach are the most beguiling aspects of Santa Barbara for the vacationer, and I will return to their playground aspects. But there are other things to see, too, downtown, around the mission, and around the city on a scenic drive.

Start by settling in. Accommodations cluster in two main

locations. One is along the oceanfront Cabrillo Boulevard, and eastward to where the luxurious Santa Barbara Biltmore resort hotel edges the Montecito shore (see Chapter 11). The other is the State Street motel row, west of downtown and east of the freeway.

LOOKING AROUND DOWNTOWN

Then explore the city center, for there the Santa Barbara flavor is most vivid.

A good place to start is the chamber of commerce (open on weekdays) at Victoria and Santa Barbara streets. Here you can pick up a map of downtown on which is plotted the "Red Tile Tour," a walk of less than 1½ miles through the three by six-block Old Town *(Pueblo Viejo)* district — where visitor interest is greatest and city building controls tightest. The chamber of commerce intersection is at one corner of that rectangle.

It's not just your usual downtown, or your usual historical walk. You pass through a cityscape of unusual continuity, for the city was well on its way to a self-imposed Spanish Colonial image when the 1925 earthquake fortuitously shook down a good many non-conforming structures of more Victorian persuasion. Architectural control ever since has produced a kind of earth-toned, tile-roof style, pervasive but by no means uniform.

Indeed, you can pick out characteristics from five distinct periods in the city's history, including the present.

The oldest is the Spanish, and two adobes show the period's tell-tale narrow rooms — limited by available beam lengths — and steep-pitched roofs. These houses are beside and across the street (Canon Perdido) from the excavation of the *presidio* (garrison), just west of Santa Barbara Street. Imagine the city when the presidio was new; it was just grassland between the foot of the mountains and the sea, with only a scattering of tiny houses.

Then imagine the more populous Mexican times. Five adobes from 1826 to 1840 remain to demonstrate that era's wider rooms and gentler roof pitches (they had found some timber for longer beams in the mountains). These traits continued, even after the American period began, in adobes built as late as 1855.

Little evidence remains of Victorian days, but abundant structures from the second two decades of this century do much to set the tone of the city. That was a heady time of building and rebuilding, when the early adobe models were no longer grand enough, and the good citizens turned to the glory of Spain. Then they were creating "antiquities" (though with modern plumbing). Now, after half a century these Roaring Twenties confections have become historical in their own right.

The most extraordinary building in town is at Anacapa and Anapamu streets: the 1929 County Courthouse. Think of the civic pride — on the eve of the Depression — that went into this "Spanish-Moorish" extravaganza spread along two sides of an entire block. (The rest is parklike lawn and trees — an unconsciously Anglo-Saxon touch far beyond the water resources of the arid Iberian Peninsula.) Note its tower, arches, painted ceilings, sculpture, tile, urns, wrought-iron lanterns, paneled doors, elaborate gates.

It's the kind they don't build anymore, and it is a mistake to assume you can get its message just by looking at the outside. Nothing can prepare you for the spaces inside, the great halls, curving staircases, galleries, and the climactic frescoed mural room. Also, be sure to take the elevator to the high tower for the view out over the city from the mountains to the sea.

Another 1920's (but pre-earthquake) marvel is El Paseo. It also covers a large part of a block: from Anacapa through to State Street, backing the De La Guerra and Oreña adobes on De La Guerra Street. Inside is the famous Street in Spain, a pedestrian way — with awnings, fountain, and outdoor eating places — onto which open a good many shops. The building also contains interior shop-lined passages and a large courtyard restaurant.

A newer adobe (1965) is the Historical Society Museum, at De La Guerra and Santa Barbara Streets. Its treasures span all phases of the city's history, including the Chinatown period. And its sheltered patio is surfaced in tamped earth and planted sparingly with a few trees and vines. This makes it much more authentic in its look backward than many gardens of missions and old adobes that have become overgrown through modern irrigation.

Santa Barbara's newest alteration of its civic visage is a remodeled State Street. The operation involved removing parking from this main artery and placing it in landscaped lots behind the stores (first 90 minutes free). Then the sidewalks were turned into promenades that became a pleasure to walk, graced as they are by benches, fountains, and plantings of shrubs and trees — now grown full enough to give the street a shaded and softened look.

Shopping and window shopping are agreeable and unpressured, and a number of eating places beckon you to tarry — either on the street, or seen as tables in open courtyards set back from the street.

A walk up State Street brings you to the art museum at the corner of Anapamu. Remodeled and enlarged from a 1914 post office, it is now a handsome gallery complex that displays some notable works, especially ancient sculpture and American painting.

THE MISSION AND MISSION CANYON

The town grew up around the presidio. The Franciscan fathers located their mission apart, where there was not only water but a suitably protective distance between their innocent neophytes and the rough, often reprehensible doings of the soldiers. Today, the mission is very much in town, though outside of downtown.

The mission occupies a commanding site looking over city and sea and out to the islands. One of the most refined in design in all the mission chain, it has a stone facade (restored and reinforced) modeled after the work of the Roman architect Vitruvius, and is unusual for having two identical towers.

It's a real step backward in time. Take the tour, look in on the secluded cloister and the dim interior of the church — with its high Moorish windows — and walk through the still cemetery to one side.

Remnants of the mission's water and water-driven works are still to be seen on and near the premises — the fountain and laundry in front, ruins of a grist mill nearby. To find the source, you must make your way up forested Mission Canyon, down which a rock-lined flume brought water from a dam.

But first a short detour, just up the canyon, at the charming natural history museum, also in a patioed Spanish Revival building from the Twenties. It displays the story of the earth around Santa Barbara and its rocks, of the Indians, and of the creatures of land, sea, and air. You will see a field of poppies perpetually in bloom indoors, and get a look at the skeleton of the mammoth — an Ice Age animal that evolved down to a dwarf (relatively speaking) out on the islands. It's not

Mission Santa Barbara occupies wooded site in Mission Canyon

just for kids — though they come by the busload.

Then again heading for the mission dam, continue on up the canyon (follow signs where the route jogs right at Foothill Road) to the botanic garden, one of the few gardens in California devoted to plants that grow in California. Its pleasures are mostly esthetic, unless you are a botanist, and include shady groves of oaks, sycamores, and coast redwoods and open meadows that are flower-strewn in spring. There are inviting spots for a rest on a bench, and even a simple picnic, and the tall mission dam — long since filled up behind with stream-borne rock and gravel — is prominent in the upper canyon.

Also notable is the Channel Islands garden, where you see plants that, over the ages in the even, sea-tempered island climate, have evolved much less than their relatives on the mainland — where more radical changes in climate took place.

THE SCENIC DRIVE AND BIKEWAY

Most of the downtown area is along Santa Barbara's Scenic Drive, marked with signs and shown on the same map as the Red Tile Tour. The natural history museum and the botanic garden are on an extension of it, mapped but not signed. Take the tour now, for an orientation circuit of the city.

From the mission the route heads easterly along the foothills to Montecito (where the map shows another unsigned loop). Then it moves down toward the sea, still in Montecito. After a jog inland, it passes two places back in Santa Barbara and just inland from the beach: The Andree Clark Bird Refuge is a marshy lake that attracts a sizeable resident and migrant bird population. And the Child's Estate zoological garden attracts kids with its animals (some of them pettable and some feedable), its playground, and its miniature train ride.

Then the route parallels the beachfront park along Cabrillo Boulevard as far as the harbor. Beyond, the drive ascends hills west of town for a passage beside Shoreline Park. Then it swings inland, passes the entrance to Arroyo Burro Beach, and circles through the Hope Ranch residential area back to town via State Street.

The section from the bird sanctuary to Shoreline Park is an excellent bikeway marked by signs — scenic and well used by cyclists.

ON THE BEACH

The highlight of the Scenic Drive is the seashore. It can also be the highlight of a stay in Santa Barbara, for it is the city's major recreational resource. This comes in three parts: the beach and the swimming, the boating facilities, and places inland but associated with the shore.

The beach is sandy and gentle of surf (protected as it is on the windward side by the harbor and its breakwater). Here are the sunning and the swimming, backed up inland by a strip of grassy park for strolling, planted in tall fan palms and bordered by the bikeway. There is also a salt water swimming pool, open in summer.

The harbor is tucked in at the west end of the beach, a shelter for perhaps seven hundred craft, picturesque with fishing boats, pleasure craft, and even with the more workaday vessels that service off-shore drilling platforms. You can walk the seawall and the breakwater, past a fish market, a bait and tackle shop, and the ticket window for the shoreline tour boat *Shirley-Ann* and fishing party boats (both may see migrating gray whales close up in winter and early spring). And you can launch, rent, or charter a boat.

Just inland is a row of motels and restaurants facing the beach, and inland a little more is an assortment of unusual things to see. Besides the bird refuge and Child's Estate, there is the Santa Barbara Winery (with a tasting room) at 202 Anacapa Street, the enormous and famous Moreton Bay fig tree by the train station at Chapala and Montecito Streets, the Carriage Museum with its collection of antiquities at 129 Castillo Street, and the Fernald and Trussell-Winchester houses at 414 W. Montecito Street.

Yosemite Falls is highest of the dozen or so to fall over valley walls

Chapter 6:

Yosemite

FEW PLACES IN THE WORLD have such a profound emotional impact on the viewer as the valley of Yosemite.

There are doubtless deeper chasms, even in the Sierra, and bigger ones. And I've seen similarly noble prospects in the Alps and in the Andes, such as the gorge of the Urubamba below Machu Picchu. But nowhere does such an architectural combination of flat valley floor and granite walls half a mile to 4,000 feet high — straight or sculptured into stirring forms and brought to life with plumes of white water plummeting over the brink — come together so dramatically and at such a scale. You are set down in the midst of grandeur, and it strikes you as being at once cosmic but not so immense you can't relate to it — the way the Grand Canyon sometimes affects people.

Seldom does the overworked adjective "breathtaking" really apply to a view. But the sight of the valley when you emerge from the long Wawona Tunnel on the road in from the south and west can accurately be so described. And seldom is an "Inspiration Point" — where you stop for that view — so accurately named. Indeed, that valley vista, with the awesome cliff of El Capitan on the left and Bridalveil Falls on the right and Half Dome in the distance beyond, ranks with Mt. Fuji, the Matterhorn, the Pyramids, the Taj Mahal, and a handful of other places as one of the visual wonders of the planet.

Once you have had that experience, the remainder of the valley becomes a progression of individual marvels.

On the north wall, Yosemite Falls — east of El Capitan — drops from higher than any of the half-dozen spectacular ones in the valley, 2,425 feet. Then the monuments are such configurations as Royal Arches, Washington Column, North Dome, and others that merit names.

On the south wall are the towering Cathedral Rocks, Sentinel Dome (above and back) and Glacier Point — once the site of a lodge and still a prime trail and road destination.

Then comes the side canyon down through which the valley's stream, the Merced River, drops over Nevada and Vernal falls, in a passage behind the most spectacular monument of all, the great polished granite bulk of Half Dome. The sheer vertical wall of this eminence faces the upper extension of the valley, watered by Tenaya Creek and here losing its vertical walls to become more like the landscapes of the High Sierra beyond. The rounded crest of Clouds Rest is the last large landmark above.

The Merced River winds through the center of the valley. Bridging it are roads that connect the main north and south roads.

The north road is the one you come in on from Merced on Highway 140 (or from farther north on Highway 120, which is not kept open in winter, as the other two access roads are). This takes you through the Arch Rock entrance, location of an old-time transportation display that includes a rail depot, rail engines and cars, and an early snow plow.

Then well into the valley you come to the settlements: Yosemite Village (site of Yosemite Lodge, with its hotel rooms and other accommodations), the national park headquarters (near Yosemite Creek, down from the falls close above), the visitor center (with its museum displays and a wildflower garden where there are summer demonstrations of the Indians' uses of native plants for food, fiber and medicine) and finally the grand old Ahwahnee Hotel — refurbished in 1977 shortly after its fiftieth birthday.

The south road — Highway 41 — comes in from Fresno through the Wawona Tunnel, mentioned above. It reaches only one major settlement, near its end at Curry Village, a visitor-service complex that includes cabins and housekeeping tents among its facilities.

Traffic and the press of crowds of people severely taxed the capacity of the park and strained its sense of amenity by the 1960's, leading to several corrective measures. One was the elaborate, long-range general management plan, still perhaps a year from fruition at this writing in 1978. But two others — limits on camping and on car traffic — were more immediate and produced some favorable results.

You are now encouraged to leave your car, especially in summer, and use public trams. Or walk, or ride a bike; there are plenty for rent. Tram lines serve areas that once were the most congested. They run from the Ahwahnee to Yosemite Lodge, from the grocery store at Yosemite Village to Curry Village, and from Curry Village to the east part of the valley — now closed to cars — as far as evanescent Mirror Lake (usually dry by fall).

Some of the intensive-use problems have thus been eased in the summer, but not all. It can still be hot and sometimes dusty. And pollutants can be trapped in the nearly closed air basin of the valley. These come from within the valley or the nearby San Joaquin Valley (which gets them from as far upwind as the Bay Area).

For these and other reasons I recommend the intermediate seasons, if you can go then, instead of summer. April, if the snow has cleared, and May, for sure, are all fresh greenery and tumbling, swollen streams and booming waterfalls — which will shrink by midsummer and may dry up altogether by the end of summer. And autumn is often seductive with its warm stillness and the gold of oaks catching the sunlight against the dark green of pines or the shade of valley walls. Perhaps best of all, the crowds are noticeably absent. Even winter has its charm, though your movements are restricted.

Once you have done the valley floor, the place to go is up. You can do this on foot or by motor.

On foot you can explore the south wall by a pair of trails that connect Glacier Point with two valley locations. Both trails are sufficiently long and steep that they are probably best as one-way walks, for which you should probably go to Glacier Point by bus and walk back or arrange a car shuttle with family or friends for a drive to or from Glacier Point. Neither is for the beginner, so I'll omit advice on maps, shoes, and other gear.

The longer of the two is called the Panorama Trail. A little more than 8 miles in length, it connects Glacier Point with Happy Isles. This is also trailhead for shorter hikes over part of the same trail to Vernal and Nevada falls and for the John Muir Trail, which reaches into the High Sierra. Note that the lower part of the route is aptly named the Mist Trail, and you should be prepared to keep your camera and yourself dry from the spray of the falls. If you are physically up to it, I recommend you make this a climb rather than a descent. On the climb you see gradually unfold one of the park's grander panoramas, culminating in the genuinely thrilling spectacle of the High Sierra seen from Glacier Point.

The other path, called the Four Mile Trail, is probably better as a descent (despite the way your leg muscles will feel the next day). It comes right down the south wall to a point near where Sentinel Creek reaches the valley floor, a little over 2 miles west of Curry Village. Its views of the valley vertically down and the falls across the way are reason enough for the trip.

Motor routes take you to uplands in park areas beyond the valley.

UPLANDS SOUTH OF THE VALLEY

To get to the southern areas, take the road through the Wawona Tunnel and up into pine forest. As Wawona Road, it leads to Wawona and beyond to Fresno. But first a digression.

At a junction a few miles from the tunnel, turn left (easterly) on a course parallel to Yosemite Valley to Glacier Point.

If you didn't get to this vantage point on foot, you must come up by car or bus, for literally and figuratively it is one of the high points of the park. Your view is down into the vast depth of the forest-carpeted valley and across it toward such sights as Yosemite Falls, east up glaciated Tenaya Canyon, to majestic Half Dome and past it, up past the prominent Vernal and Nevada waterfalls to Little Yosemite Valley — and beyond all to the serrated crest of the High Sierra.

On the way to Glacier Point you pass a side road and two trails.

The road leads a short distance to Badger Pass, site of a ski lodge open Thanksgiving through Easter, usually, served by bus from Yosemite Lodge. With three double chair lifts, two T-bars, and a rope tow, it is a popular downhill ski area as well as starting point for ski touring. It also has a snow play area. Beyond, the road to Glacier Point opens after the snows are over, generally in May, sometimes in April, and closes with the first heavy snowfall in autumn.

Then you come to the 13-mile Pohono Trail. It parallels Yosemite Valley beyond, though above and back from the cliffs, then works its way down to the valley floor near Bridalveil Falls by way of a vista point called Tunnel View. The

Upper valley reflects in still waters of Merced River overflow pool

second trail is a short one to the summit of Sentinel Dome, famous for having the park's most photographed tree — a wind-flattened Jeffrey pine — and a panoramic high-country view.

Back on Wawona Road, head south to the resort of Wawona, beside the South Fork of the Merced River. A bit of Victoriana that dates from the great hotel era of the 1880's, the hotel's original and later sections have been modernized; half have baths. The hotel is open from Memorial Day weekend through October. Its well-kept grounds include a golf course, tennis, and other facilities, and horses can be hired.

Close by, an 1858 wooden covered bridge signals the Pioneer Yosemite History Center. This is a collection of antique buildings — a stone jail, log cabins, other structures — moved here and reassembled as a kind of village fitted out with antique wagons and other horse-drawn conveyances.

Then beyond (south) on Wawona Road is the turnoff to Mariposa Grove, one of the Sierra's finer stands of sequoias, or big trees, and one of the chief reasons for the creation of the park.

It was the second half of the nineteenth century, the era of extermination, when animal species (including the California grizzly bear) were vanishing from the earth and giant sequoias, largest plants on earth, were being felled for such trivial uses as grapestakes. John Muir and others trumpeted the threat throughout the land, and as a result President Lincoln set aside the federal lands that included Yosemite Valley and the Mariposa Grove in 1864 as a state park. Then for further protection the national park was created in 1890 surrounding the state park reservation — and the two were merged as one federal unit in 1906.

Today the grove is as awe-inspiring and temple-like as it was when it moved Muir to lofty sentiment. Coastal redwoods may be taller (big trees reach 300 feet or so) and Bristlecone pines — over in the White Mountains, east of the Sierra — may be older, but for ponderous majesty these trees have no equal. The patriarch Grizzly Giant is thought to be the oldest one here, perhaps 2,700 years. And it is very likely the fastest-growing, demonstrating extraordinary vigor for an organism so huge and so ancient.

Cars are no longer permitted within the grove. You park and walk, or take one of the trams that run at periods when visitors are expected.

UPLANDS NORTH OF THE VALLEY

In this direction there are fewer motor destinations than to the south. The passage gets you into some higher country, though, sampling what the back country is like for hikers. This includes crossing the Sierra crest at 9,941-foot Tioga Pass and the steep descent of the rugged and arid east slope.

To get there, take the Big Oak Flat Road out of the valley, then turn onto Tioga Road. It passes through superlative coniferous forest, with access along the way to a number of camps and trailheads — including one route over to Yosemite Falls and beside it down the north wall to the valley floor. You also pass the road to White Wolf Lodge (cabins, tents, dining hall) at trailhead for the Tuolumne River valley.

And you come close to the May Lake High Sierra Camp, one of eight tented camps on a 65-mile trail circuit that provide board and lodging for hikers and horseback riders. (Reservations, as for all park accommodations, must be made through Yosemite Park and Curry Co.).

Finally, beautiful Tuolumne Meadows is a huge open grassland, laced by sparkling streams and ringed by granite ridges, high enough to be near the tree line. It is a center of camping activity and site of a lodge (tent cabins, dining hall), and starting point for the High Sierra Camp circuit as well as for hikes farther into the mountains on the John Muir Trail. The park service makes an effort to have the road — including Tioga Pass immediately to the east — open by the Memorial Day weekend; facilities close in September.

Palm Canyon is a touch of natural desert at fringe of civilization

Chapter 7:

Palm Springs and the Low Desert

THE DESERT ALWAYS surprises newcomers, who mostly expect to see the movie cliché of endless sand dunes. Instead, the desert — at least in California — is simply territory inland from mountains that wring all the rainfall out of Pacific storms. It is thus a land of plants and animals that adapt to dryness, and a place of low humidity (except during summer thunderstorm episodes).

The desert comes in two parts. Low desert is around sea level or below, high desert is usually upwards of 2,000 feet or so in elevation. Each has its characteristic, sometimes sparse, plant cover, its wildflowers, and — if you react the way I do — its own special charm.

In the low desert winters are warm and spring and fall are equable, while summers are downright hot. The high desert is cooler, and may even experience snow in winter. The low desert is where the winter resort communities flourish — their season much extended in these days of air conditioning.

Once that resort area was just Palm Springs, marvel of the Coachella Valley for its warmth in winter, green lawns, palms, and above all, its number of swimming pools — close to the 6,000 mark.

With concern for its image, this bustling village at the base of the mighty San Jacinto Mountains achieved an unusually well-groomed cityscape by means of landscaping (and night-lighting on the palms of its main street), sign control and other restrictions — including a limit on height of buildings. It attracted enough well-off visitors that in their wake came shops of national renown, some of them outposts of

New York. Fine hotels flourished and some fine restaurants — though not many could survive the severe fluctuations between winter crowds and summer doldrums.

Now there is still Palm Springs, but it is like the nucleus of a comet — its tail a resort and recreation area that has pushed south and east, with ever lower density, as far as Indio.

Palm Springs still has the great concentration of hotels, lodges, and resorts (note that none bears so crass a designation as "motel"). And it does — literally — fill up on weekends and holidays during the November through Memorial Day season. Reservations are always desirable. If you need help finding accommodations, write the Palm Springs Convention and Visitors Bureau, Municipal Airport Terminal, Palm Springs 92262, or telephone (714) 327-8411.

The new territory beyond has hotels and resorts, too. Some of the resorts are condominium and country club developments. The golf course count tells the story of the spread: six 18-hole and five 9-hole courses in Palm Springs, twenty-three 18-hole and six 9-hole courses beyond.

Country clubs account for a majority of the golf courses, but there are many public ones and enough hotels have guest club memberships that there is no lack of opportunity to play.

Likewise, of the twenty-two tennis court locations, more than half are in the new area and in country clubs, but five hotels or resorts have their own and there are three public locations in Palm Springs — one with nine courts and ten practice lanes. There are nearly 300 courts in the area.

So Palm Springs and its neighbors form one of the prime playgrounds of California, and the typical vacation there is heavily devoted to urban outdoor recreation by day — if no more strenuous than soaking up sun — perhaps to doing the night spots after the sun goes down (in season).

Besides the ubiquitous swimming pool, hotels now commonly offer facilities ranging from saunas and whirlpool baths all the way up to the elaborate hot mineral-water pools, steam rooms, and other services of the Palm Springs Spa Hotel — built on the site of the springs that gave the city its name.

Some lodgings also have putting greens, and such things as racquetball courts are turning up. And a good many places have bicycles for their guests. Palm Springs has a 13½-mile bikeway, but apart from recreation, the congestion of 1½ million visitors a year — mostly car-borne — makes the bike a practical device for getting around town.

VISITOR ATTRACTIONS IN THE CITY

There are four major visitor facilities, all on or just off the main artery of Palm Canyon Drive. All charge admission. Inquire when you get to town about days and hours they are open.

The northernmost is the famous tramway, its well-marked entrance on Tramway Drive is one of the most prominent sights seen by people driving in on State Highway 111 from the direction of Los Angeles.

The access road climbs 3,000 feet to the foot of the tramway — an elevation gain you hardly notice until you look back at the sea-level desert floor receding behind. Then it's a fifteen or twenty-minute ride, in operation every day from November through May, mid-morning through early evening.

The two cars counterweight each other, and they pass midway in a lift that reaches 8,516 feet atop one of the great mountain scarps of Western America. You gain an altitude equivalent in climate change to moving from Mexico to Canada — as you can see in changing plant complexes. And the temperature at the top is a bracing 40° cooler than on the desert below. This means you should take along a jacket even in summer, and expect snow in winter. You can rent equipment for snow play then, and the wilderness beyond attracts snow campers and cross-country skiers.

You alight in mountain forest. Then you can simply stay around the Mountain Station, which has a view terrace and a restaurant that serves luncheon and dinner, or you can stroll about on the cool, pine-scented slopes — perhaps over to a dramatic desert view point not far away.

Or, with advance preparation, you can go hiking. An obvious goal is 10,804-foot Mt. San Jacinto, six miles away. For hiking and for backpack camping (campgrounds are nearby) you need a wilderness permit. You can take a chance on picking one up at the ranger station near the tramway, or write in advance to, Mt. San Jacinto Wilderness State Park, P.O. Box 308, Idyllwild, CA 93349, or telephone (714) 659-2607.

The second in-town magnet is the Palm Springs Desert Museum, at 101 Museum Drive, in the center of town a long block west of Palm Canyon Drive. The handsome building houses displays of art and of desert natural history and has an auditorium for music and drama. It rises out of a moat-like sunken garden adorned with some dramatic pieces of contemporary sculpture.

The third visitor target is a rare touch of desert in this oasis community, the 40-year-old Moorten Botanical Garden, on South Palm Canyon Drive — just south of where the main street curves to become East Palm Canyon. Here on four acres you can wander among more than 2,000 kinds of desert plants from the world over, grouped by area where they originated.

And the fourth attraction is still farther south on Palm Canyon Drive, past the toll gate of the Agua Caliente Indian Reservation.

Called the Indian Canyons because they are mostly within the reservation, Palm Canyon and its tributary Andreas and Murray canyons beckon with the largest stands of native California fan palms anywhere. Relict from an earlier age of tropical climate, these desert trees now survive only in oases where there is surface or underground water all year. So dense are they in places that they dim the light, with only an occasional sunbeam penetrating the green crowns and past the shaggy tan thatch of spent fronds — or blackened trunks where fire has consumed dry fronds that otherwise would hide the trunks. The canyons are closed from as early as May through mid-October because of fire hazard.

Palm forest, a picnic area, a stream (which may falter as summer approaches in dry years), and rugged rocks mark Andreas Canyon, the destination of a short side road. And from there a trail reaches over to the similar landscapes of Murray Canyon. You can walk a mile or so up each canyon without difficulty.

Road ends at Hermit's Bench, on a rise overlooking the principal groves in the main part of Palm Canyon, where there is also a picnic area. About two miles of trail take you upstream, past rush-ringed ponds and a creek that flows during the winter and during snow-melt in the high country, to where passage becomes nearly impossible at some dry falls (or wet when the stream is up). If the information sheet you get at the entrance still blithely suggests the "easy" walk to Ribbonwood on State Highway 74 up in the highlands, forget it; it's a slow and arduous hike of 14 miles.

IN SEARCH OF LOW DESERT

Then looking for real desert beyond the edge of irrigated greenery, you first must head east and southeast on State Highway 111, through two kinds of development unique in California. One blends into the other: condo and country-club suburbia and desert agriculture that extends well beyond Indio.

In Palm Desert, halfway along, you will find an excellent place for a desert briefing at the Living Desert Reserve about 1½ miles south of Highway 111 on Portola Road.

Here you see an assemblage of birds, animals, and reptiles of the low desert (technically the Colorado Desert). This includes nocturnals (creatures active at night) displayed in a darkened hall so they are awake and moving about. And here are plants from the low desert and from other North American deserts — among them the nearby high desert, with its Joshua trees and Mojave yuccas.

The reserve occupies 1,000 acres, and you can explore the lowlands and the flanks of Eisenhower Mountain on six miles of trail. You can look in on bighorn sheep (the only reliable place to see them in California outside a zoo) in a research enclosure. There are also a walk-through, free-flight aviary next to and partly enclosing a palm oasis, a plant nursery, an animal hospital, halls for meetings and exhibits, and a picnic area. The reserve is open 9 to 5 every day, September through May.

DATE GROVES AND DESERT PARKS

Then heading east, look for exotic agriculture on the way to three Riverside County parks that offer good samplings of the desert: Lake Cahuilla, Indio Palms, and Mecca Hills. (Note that the second two have no water, so be sure to take along a good supply. And they are for you only if the idea of back country is not dismaying; they are not parks in the city-park sense).

Lofty date palm groves, their dark interiors evocative of Egyptian temples, are the first and most spectacular evidence of desert agriculture. Their fruit is harvested mainly from October through December. You'll see groves from Palm Desert nearly to the Salton Sea, but two retail establishments that make the most provision for visitors — Shields and Sniff's date gardens — are located on Highway 111 just east of Jefferson Street (west of Indio).

Also look for vineyards, fields, orchards, and other produce fresh at roadside, including some kind of citrus all year, melons in spring through fall, and pomegranates in the winter. Grapefruit, for which the valley is famous, come from trees often planted as an understory in date groves.

Lake Cahuilla is the closest park, about 5½ miles south of Highway 111 on Jefferson Street. The lake, part of the Coachella Valley irrigation system, is stocked with trout for fishermen in the cool winter months. The grounds have picnic tables amid lawns, with date palms transplanted from a grove that was subdivided. Trails reach back into the mountains, affording some expansive views over the valley. The shoreline of the Lake Cahuilla that filled the valley in ancient times is clearly visible on mountain slopes above the present lake.

To get to Indio Palms, turn north on Washington Street (also west of Indio) from either Highway 111 or the I-10 freeway. The entrance, about 5 miles north of the freeway, has a gate to keep cars out, but you can walk in for perhaps a quarter mile on a dirt road to Hidden Palms, first of a chain of oases that marks the path of the great San Andreas Fault along the Indio Hills.

From road-end a half-mile trail leads over to the brink of an arroyo overlooking the palms of Pushawalla Oasis. You can work your way down into the canyon and explore among the green trees, which extend for perhaps a mile. Water is visible here and there, but exists mostly underground. You pass mesquite thickets and some wildly deformed rock canyon walls.

To get to Mecca Hills, follow Highway 111 southeast to Mecca, then turn east on Box Canyon Road. Just after crossing the Coachella Canal, about 4 miles east of town, turn left on a dirt road that in 2 miles ends in Painted Canyon. The park contains a nearly treeless system of canyons vigorously sculptured into the Mecca Hills. This is also on the San Andreas Fault, which accounts for contorted formations in the colorful, hardened ancient muds. You can explore any of a dozen side canyons off the 8-mile-long main canyon, fascinating just for their variety of form and color and sense of aloneness.

HIGH DESERT SIDE TRIP

The Mecca Hills park is well on the way into a full-day loop trip (for another day) through a wholly different kind of desert: the high southern edge of the Mojave. For this one get an early start, and east of Mecca just follow Box Canyon Road northeast through the Mecca Hills and across I-10 to the southern entrance to a half-million-acre gem of high desert: Joshua Tree National Monument.

As you ascend to nearly 3,000 feet at the Cottonwood entrance station, you leave behind ironwood and other low-desert plants for landscapes of juniper and Mojave yucca. At Cottonwood there is a palm oasis and a campground, and water.

Then you descend somewhat to cross part of the vast Pinto Basin before climbing up to the 4,000-foot central plateau. Notable along the way are a thick stand of ocotillo and an extraordinarily dense stand of cholla cactus — some of them an unusual eight feet tall.

A leveling and numerous splashes of white rock announce the upland. At a junction you can go right and down to the National Monument headquarters at Twentynine Palms — useful for information and orientation about the monument — before returning to continue through the central area.

Or, you can go left along the main road. You shortly enter the monument's decidedly histrionic settings, with passages through Joshua trees as thick as if in forests, their arms in weirdly supplicating postures, backed by ramparts of quartz monzonite bouldered outcrops — as authentically Old West a scene as anything in California.

Allow plenty of time so you can stop at such highlights as Keys View, up in the piñon-juniper woodland — nearly a mile above the Coachella Valley, and spectacular on a clear day — Hidden Valley, and other notable sights in the well-named Wonderland of Rocks area. Most are marked by discreet signs along the road. Note that here, too, water is scarce or non-existent, so carry a good supply.

The main monument road comes out in the community of Joshua Tree, and from there you can return to the low desert on State Highway 62 via Yucca Valley.

Giant Pelton wheels are still to be seen at mine works near Jackson

Chapter 8:

Gold Country

THIS IS A ROLLING vacation along State Highway 49. One of California's several specialty routes (those through the redwoods and past the missions are other examples), it is probably the shortest and most concentrated in interest of all.

Named for the Forty-Niners of the Gold Rush that did so much to populate California, the road is a literal bonanza of seven major Gold Country towns, along with a goodly number of smaller towns, relics, and sites — from the Mother Lode to the Northern Mines. In them the past is still prominently apparent.

The distance from the southern end at Oakhurst to Nevada City is about 220 miles. To the highway's far northern end — through Downieville and beyond — it is nearly 300 miles.

On this kind of vacation you spend as much time as suits your fancy in interesting towns, and explore such side trips as seem promising. You can see the highlights presented in this chapter on a three-day visit without undue exertion. And the journey might inspire you to a more detailed exploration later on.

Two items of planning are in order. Accommodations are adequate though not plentiful, so especially in summertime you should try to plan your overnights and seek advance motel reservations (several guides list and grade them). And if you would like to drive the side roads, write down the turn-off points in advance; most of the roads are two-laned, not prominently marked, and easy to overshoot.

Two traits of the highway come as a surprise to first-time visitors. One is the unexpected variety of the topography, and the other is the unexpected variety of the landscape.

The road is seldom level and seldom straight. And though these are officially the Sierra "foothills," the landforms exhibit dramatic heights and slopes of truly mountainous scale. You cross a series of relatively gentle uplands separated by canyons and deep gorges, down the walls of which and then up again the road wends at an often slow pace. One of the most impressive of such chasms is the gorge of the Merced River between Bear Valley and Coulterville. Another is the North Fork of the American River — crossed by a soaring high bridge for the I-50 freeway, just east of Auburn.

Though there are only a few plant communities present, the landscape still manages a continually changing appearance, largely the result of frequent changes in altitude (which varies from about 1,000 to a little over 2,500 feet, mostly).

You pass through the lower edge of yellow pine forest (represented mainly by ponderosa pine), digger pine and oak woodland, chaparral, and grassland. Much of the latter is bucolic ranchland cleared for grazing, sometimes picturesquely strewn with boulders. Some of the slopes have evidently been stripped by logging (or by fire), and you encounter sawmills and logging trucks from time to time.

Hillsides are emerald with grass from late fall through spring; the hot summer sun turns them — appropriately enough — to gold. Spring brings out wildflowers and fall a surprising (for California) show of leaf color, usually climaxing in November.

Towns in the Gold Country bear some resemblances to one another. They are likely to be linear, for example, with a business district along a main street in a canyon bottom. On side hills you find houses, perhaps a church or two, and maybe the cemetery. The older houses will be of two generations, early Greek Revival in style, and later, more ornate Victorians. The churches will probably be both white and steepled.

And a hill may hold a courthouse, for the highway passes through eight county seats. (Among the earliest formed, the counties are smaller and thus more numerous than elsewhere in California.) All this makes for an unusual collection of courthouses — mainly antique, some quite splendidly pretentious in the style of the day.

Down in town, probably few wooden houses are left, for fire was a frequent hazard during the wooden (and tent) phases of the gold towns. The second generation of buildings used adobe or stone, both abundant, and then brick. These masonry buildings often had solid iron shutters as a fire-protection measure. Today enough of these structures — often false-fronted, sometimes with roofs that shelter boardwalks — remain to give many gold towns a distinctly nineteenth century frontier flavor. And note that the best parts of some gold towns are a block or two from the highway.

Three specialties widespread in the Gold Country add color to a visit: Nearly every town or hamlet has antique shops, more than a dozen towns have old hotels or inns where you can stay in restored surroundings (though the bathroom is probably down the hall), and at least ten — from Oakhurst north — offer theater productions, playing mostly in summertime.

And of course there are the museums to be expected in an area of so much history. These range from whole towns to mines to Indian sites, restored or reconstructed — as at Columbia, Coloma, Indian Grinding Rock, Malakoff Diggins (without the "g"), and Empire Mine state historic parks. Many of the county seats have museums; the one in Jackson is notable for its location in a fine old house. Elsewhere a historical society or chamber of commerce may sponsor the museum; the museum in Grass Valley is notable for its collection of mining gear. (Note some museums are open only in summer, some only on weekends.)

And isolated artifacts abound: steam locomotives from mine-tunnel size to standard gauge, ore cars, Conestoga and freight wagons, mine headframes and stamp mills.

I like some of the big towns best, I think, despite traffic and parking problems. They tend to offer the greatest numbers of treasures and the most exploring for your money, so to speak. My nominations: Sonora, Jackson, Placerville, Auburn, and Nevada City.

Some of the small ones are good to stop in, too: Coulterville, with its really antique look; Jamestown and Mokelumne Hill — both detours off Highway 49; Columbia, gem of the Gold Country (at least the part preserved in the park); the time-turned-back town of Murphys; Coloma, the non-town preserved in a park; Downieville, northerly and somnolent.

Highway 49 actually begins at Oakhurst, on the Highway 41 access road to Yosemite — the direct route for Southern Californians. But since there is little except pleasant country on the first segment, readers from other parts of California might best start at Mariposa, on Highway 140, the main Yosemite access road.

MARIPOSA is of middling size, and except for its location perhaps not the most felicitous introduction to the Gold Country — for its older relics seem almost overwhelmed by the new. Nevertheless, it has a scattering of gems — old St. Joseph's church as a monument for travelers arriving from the south; a brick IOOF hall and John Trabucco's warehouse, among others, on the main street; a stone jail a block up the hill on Bullion Street, and the nifty old (1854) Mariposa County Courthouse (one of the more restrained of Golden Age courthouses) on the same street. There are also an outdoor theater and a museum.

The side trip to Hornitos — 13 miles from Mt. Bullion (north of Mariposa), then 11 miles back to the highway at Bear Valley — is probably a better choice than the main highway. It has an unusually rich collection of ruins and survivors from the old days.

COULTERVILLE, the next Highway 49 stop, is tiny and obviously a remnant, its rural setting mostly uncluttered by the recent development that mars the antiquity of many gold towns. Noteworthy here are the Jeffery Hotel (with a few guest rooms) and the adjoining Magnolia Saloon and museum. Also visible are Coulter's Hotel (the town's first), a Wells Fargo building, an IOOF-Coulterville Justice Hall building, antique shops, and a donkey engine.

Then there are two small towns, worth poking about if you have plenty of time, or by-passable if you don't. Chinese Camp has a few oldies — the post office is excellent and distinctive plantings of ailanthus, or tree of heaven, imported from China. Jamestown is a charming, almost stage-set little town you might easily miss where a bend of Highway 49 bypasses it on the approach to Sonora.

SONORA, "Queen of the Southern Mines," is definitely big city after the hamlets and open country around. There are three sections of canyon-bottom main street in the form of a Tee as Highways 49 and 108 enter town from downcanyon, then split in opposite directions (the latter off to the Sonora Pass crossing of the Sierra). Most of the interesting buildings are on the steep hill on the left as you enter: some grand old houses (a number of them restored), the chamber of commerce and museum (in the former jail), the highly visible St. Patrick's church, and the even more prominent yellow brick Tuolumne County Courthouse.

On the main street is the two-story adobe Gunn House, one of the Gold Country inns refitted for guests. And on the same street (Washington, also Highway 49) farther out is the city's most celebrated architectural work: the brick-red wooden St. James Episcopal Church, from 1859. Across the street from it, notice the elaborate real Victorian house.

COLUMBIA, "Gem of the Southern Mines," small but one of the richest of gold towns, may be the one mandatory detour off Highway 49: about 4 miles north of Sonora and just a little way off the highway. Most of the town is within the state historic park, which has done its restoration and reconstruction as of the 1850's and 1860's. It's a living museum. Many of the early commercial buildings have been re-created as exhibits with artifacts of the era, but many are "live" and in actual operation as restaurants, the nine-room City Hotel, a barbershop, shops with costumed attendants and antique merchandise, two theaters — even a stagecoach ride and a place for gold panning. And just outside town, in the direction of Sonora, don't miss the lovely little St. Anne's church.

From Columbia you have two choices: Continue on the back road, via Vallecito, to the tree-shaded island of another time called Murphys — with the restored hotel, theater, collection of stone gold-era buildings, and Victorian houses. Or, return to Highway 49 and go through Mark Twain's old stamping ground — more interesting for its history than visually. Look for the turnoff to Jackass Hill, where the Twain cabin has been restored. Note the Morgan Mine at Carson Hill. See the Twain statue (and one of a frog) at Angels Camp — setting for *The Celebrated Jumping Frog of Calaveras County.*

MOKELUMNE HILL, next requires a brief detour from the highway (marked "49 Historic"). Don't pass it by. Perhaps because the highway goes around, "Mok Hill" sometimes seems sleepier than most Gold Country towns. Like many, it is small, but its main street has an unusually fine collection of old buildings, of which the carefully restored (and operational) Hotel Leger is a beautiful example. There are also an old courthouse (from before county government moved to San Andreas in 1866), the almost inevitable IOOF building, old stores, the *Calaveras Chronicle* office (Mark Twain was a reporter), and a Congregational church.

JACKSON is the second big city along the route. And as the highway curves through it you can see the old town rising from a low main street up the customary hill — in this case crowned by an uncustomary *moderne* courthouse — to your right. Some highlights include the National Hotel (restored and in use), the unusually tall IOOF building, and the county museum up on the hill in the Brown House. Beyond the edge of town, St. Sava's Serbian Orthodox church and the Kennedy and Argonaut mines are famous.

A third detour, from Jackson, takes you 13 miles to the superbly atmospheric little town of Volcano — also with an old hotel (the St. George) and a theater. Look for the brewery, the school, the confectionery, the jail, and other veteran structures. You can return via Indian Grinding Rock State Historic Park to Highway 49 at Sutter Creek.

North of Jackson on Highway 49, several small towns are found close together: Sutter Creek, Amador City, Drytown, Plymouth. Each has its handful of memorabilia, and each has antique stores in more than usual numbers. Sutter Creek, the largest, has two inns where you can stay; Amador City also has one.

PLACERVILLE is an archetypal canyon city, with a main street that — though bypassed by a freeway off to one side — will always be congested. The place has an old-time, almost European flavor, and beyond downtown the city's houses perch often courageously amid gardens and trees on steep slopes. Placerville has some curiosities: a gold mine and stamp mill in a city park (Bedford), a county museum and a pipe organ at the county fairgrounds, a winery, a Southern Pacific locomotive.

COLOMA, over the hill about 9 miles northwest, is where it all began. Here, now mostly preserved in a state historic park, you will find the basic landmark: Sutter's Mill, where John Marshall found the first "colors" in 1848. The park and town offer other history, restored, rebuilt, or new: a museum, mining machinery displays, the Mormon cabin, iron-shuttered stone buildings, a Victorian hotel (seven rooms) and a replica of one. And there is summer theater. Nearby, look also for the scenic side road to the Marshall monument, marking his grave, and the reconstruction of the Marshall cabin.

AUBURN, athwart the I-80 freeway and the SP main line, is big and busy — until you seek out its little enclave of the past in Old Town. The imposing 1894 county courthouse is the landmark (it's one of the grander ones, and you can hardly miss it). Then down below it to the southwest is the historic section, consisting of several blocks of offices, shops, and restaurants, and the curious firehouse, shaped as if it were all tower. Also look into the county museum at the fairgrounds.

GRASS VALLEY, like Angels Camp, shows its modernity to the detriment of its antiquity. It may be more interesting for its past notables than for its ambience today: Lola Montez, the dancer who came here from Europe, and Lotta Crabtree, the budding entertainer whom La Montez encouraged, and even Josiah Royce, the philosopher. The Montez house is one of the sights, as are several other nineteenth-century structures. The North Star Powerhouse Mining Museum is perhaps the best of its kind. And the Empire Mine State Historic Park, when restored in the next few years, will be one of the great visitor magnets of the Gold Country.

NEVADA CITY, a close neighbor to Grass Valley, is one of the high spots of the Gold Country experience — with its crooked old hillside streets lined with Victoriana and pre-Victoriana, its tree-shaded Victorian residential areas, its steepled churches, its museums (one of them in a firehouse), its old accommodations (in the 1857 National Hotel and in the Carpenter's-Gothic Red Castle above town), its remnants of Chinatown, its restaurants, its antique shops and galleries, its theater. A brutal freeway right past the center of town impairs the sense of past and complicates traffic flow, but does not quite succeed in dispelling the aura of antiquity.

Nevada City is the northern terminus for most Gold Country trips, but you can continue on the route of Highway 49 up into the mountains for another 75 miles or so. It's great fall color country and you can start with a side trip to the Malakoff Diggins.

DOWNIEVILLE, small and quiet, is the jewel of this northern extension of the trip. It lacks the crowds and preoccupation with growth of some of the more southerly towns, and has aged gracefully, with an excellent collection of buildings that date back to the 1850's.

You can return from there or continue north and higher into the Sierra, crossing 6,701-foot Yuba Pass before Highway 49 ends at Highway 89 — which leads southeast toward Lake Tahoe and northwest toward Lassen Volcanic National Park.

Corkscrew track is foreground for 20-story sky jump at Knott's

Chapter 9:

Orange County Fun Factories

NORMALLY IT DOES NOT occur to me to go out to an amusement park of a Saturday afternoon or evening. Nonetheless, as a resident of a tourist region, I have been cast in the role of guide for out-of-town visitors often enough that I have come to know the local parks passing well. Where once I tended to dismiss them as just "commercial," I have gradually come to regard them as among the marvels of our time.

On such encounters I have unfailingly been agreeably surprised at the wealth of ingenuity man can devote to creating physical sensation that teeters on the edge of calamity without actually reaching it, spatial fantasies of enormous sophistication, and such curiosities on display as exotic birds and animals, old cars and planes, and artifacts from the world of film.

Of the fifteen amusement and animal parks in California (including the two major zoos), the three big parks in Orange County make up the handiest concentration, so this group is the prime target of the vacationer who seeks this special form of diversion.

(Five more parks are scattered about Los Angeles: Magic Mountain northwest of town — a pure ride and show park; Busch Bird Sanctuary in the San Fernando Valley — once an amusement park, now a bird sanctuary; Universal Studios just north of Cahuenga Pass — the great movie illusion place; Los Angeles Zoo in Griffith Park; and Marineland at Palos Verdes — the sea-animal show. Three others are in or near San Diego, and four are in northern California.)

Walt Disney didn't start the Orange County phenomenon, but his park in Anaheim, stunningly original when it opened in the 1950's, certainly put that growing edge of the Los Angeles metropolis on the map.

Disney drew on the movie industry's vast talent pool and wealth of experience in visual artifice and esoteric engineering. He fabricated the first truly plausible make-believe environments that combined physical sensation to immerse the participant. These he called "adventures," rather than merely "rides," and thus was born the "theme park." Almost overnight it outmoded the old-style amusement centers that had flourished from the nineteenth century up to the Great Depression — a kind of park that made only a halting comeback after World War II.

Around the central magnet of Disneyland grew a glittering (or sometimes merely flashy) collection of other parks, museums, side shows, and even such visitor services as a "Fun Bus," that shuttles among the attractions. Along with a clutch of hotels, the combination makes Orange County one of the permanent wonders of the tourist industry. Though much of the same has by now been erected in Florida, that sincerest form of flattery does little to diminish the appeal of the California complex for the visitor or resident.

In a real sense it is industry, and "clean" industry to boot — except for the byproducts of cars that clog the Santa Ana Freeway. And it is industry of such magnitude and variety that it takes customers considerably more than one day to make the rounds. I like to call the constituent parts "fun factories," for most of them are efficient mills for the production of that commodity.

Some of the output is musical and other stage entertainment or outdoor spectacle. Much of it is sheer visceral excitement. And though a large part of the thrill aspect is aimed at the youthful (or at least the teenage and early adult) end of the visitor spectrum, there is still plenty of less strenuous interest, too. Something for everyone in the family, so to speak, though the biggest mistake is to assume that the emphasis is on small children. For most of the parks, my advice to parents is to wait until the kids are old enough to enjoy their offerings.

If you like crowds, you can find them. And conversely, you can stay away at super-crowded times if you don't. Expect the hordes on holiday long weekends, Christmas and spring vacations, and in the summer. At both Disneyland and Knott's Berry Farm, the biggest numbers turn out over the Fourth of July.

Admission prices are too changeable and complex to detail here, but as of this writing you can expect to pay up to $10 per person for a day at one of the major parks — or maybe more, depending on how much you spend for refreshments, lunch, or other meals, and rides not included in the basic admission.

A few simple tactical rules are worth noting. Arrive early, when ticket lines are short. Do some advance research on the most popular rides so you can take them before long lines form. In some cases, make the circuit of the park in the direction least favored by the crowd. Take along reserve rations so you can eat at off-hours, again to minimize standing in line. Make sure you have a rendezvous point in case your party gets separated. Beware of the sun (take a brimmed hat or cap) even on winter days. Set a time limit on your stay to avoid exhaustion. And find a place to stay nearby, to minimize local travel and parking effort.

The list that follows is not alphabetical. It is almost (but not quite) my grading of places according to the time to be spent at each.

DISNEYLAND, Harbor Boulevard at Santa Ana Freeway, Anaheim (714) 533-4456

While most parks are rated in terms of average stay in hours, half days, or less frequently a full day, Disneyland probably requires more than one day to experience in something approaching its entirety. Number One is not the largest in area, though through meticulous planning its 77 acres contain perhaps the highest density (and thus the least walking per attraction) of any park.

With more than fifty activities, it can be a bit overwhelming the first time, so if you don't have friends who are knowing guides, try a conducted tour. The narrator can be of considerable help in mastering the lay of the land.

The Space Mountain ride, new in 1977, was the most recent major addition. Actually a sophisticated roller coaster, it puts you in a rocket craft at a space launching station, raises you with deceptive ease, and then hurtles you with electrifying sensation down through remarkable illusions of cosmic space. But notice the *caveat* that it is not for small children; even some adults find its plunging descent unnerving.

Elsewhere, as before, the park is arranged in many "lands": Frontierland, Fantasyland, and the like, beyond its

⅝-scale Main Street. It's all fantasy that started out with techniques perfected for what the camera sees to make movies then went movie sets one better: The most successful of the Disney adventures place you in the center of the action and move you through as part of a three-dimensional performance.

Pirates of the Caribbean is one of the most felicitous of such happenings, for its sets, its special effects, and its one great visceral-sensation motion surprise. And it is one of the most popular, as evidenced by long lines.

Another excellent one, the refurbished jungle ride, has no drastic motion effects, but it is a triumph of scene design, complete with such mechanical marvels as full-sized model elephants that flex their trunks.

One that I think is a gem is Small World. Though it's a fun ride in non-rocking boats, it seems to me to stumble on the threshhold of a genuine three-dimensional art form that envelops the spectator-participant in a combination of music, clockwork dance, color, and motion. And I find some of the visual effects in the Haunted Mansion to be breathtakingly splendid theater.

The whole setting is an environmental tour-de-force, with two charming elements.

One such element is the transportation fantasy, ranging from yesteryear's antique steam locomotive and horse-drawn streetcar to the monorail that circles the park and connects with the Disneyland Hotel — a mass-transit device years ahead of its time when installed in the 1950's and perhaps still so. Are the rockets, the windjammer, the autopia, and other devices all unreal? Look for your answer in 107 acres of automobiles parked beyond the entrance gate.

The other part of the environmental illusion is the physical setting, in which a gum wrapper is not suffered to remain on the ground, the landscaping is always perfectly groomed, flowers are always in bloom. It takes some doing, but the result pays off in a sense of order and well-being that keeps the crowds coming back.

There is a full program of entertainment on several stages and of spectacles on the street in the summer, and a lesser schedule at other times. Consult a newspaper for current details.

KNOTT'S BERRY FARM, 8039 Beach Boulevard, Buena Park (714) 827-1776

This one grew (from a berry farm) in less coherent fashion than Disneyland, but it grew big. Its park beginnings go back to the time when visitors needed to be entertained while they waited for Mrs. Knott's chicken dinners back Before the War. Then it rode Orange County's postwar boom successfully to become a park with a six to eight-hour rating and forty rides (plus shops, eating places, live entertainment, and a number of free attractions) spread over 150 acres. In annual attendance, it ranks after the two Disney establishments but ahead of all others in America.

There are three major parts to the park, all of them theme-related to the past, all with thrill rides: The Roaring Twenties, Fiesta Village, and Old West Ghost Town. I would visit them in that sequence, because I suspect the crowd gets to them in the reverse order.

The Roaring Twenties show-stoppers are the Corkscrew (a roller coaster with not one but two complete upside-down loops) and the 20-story Sky Jump parachutes. Good luck. The rides are modern versions of amusement park devices of the Twenties era, and they're grouped about an early airfield complete with runways, a big hangar, old planes as props, and such diversions as a motorcycle chase — plus dance pavilions and a sophisticated big theater.

Fiesta Village in the past was the least exciting, but it has been revved up with a thrill ride devised by diabolical Swiss engineers. Called a shuttle shop, it speeds you from zero to 54 miles per hour in 5 seconds, puts you through a vertical loop, then comes to a halt on an upgrade for a moment of weightlessness. Gravity then moves the car backward through the loop to another gravity-stopping point at the opposite end. Then you subside back to the start. Though the experience might seem endless, it actually takes just 29 seconds.

Also new to Fiesta Village are an Omnivision theater where you can see films of rides you may not have the courage to take in person, a refurbished animal farm, and new entertainment, shop, restaurant, and game spaces — plus a sound and light show.

The Ghost Town is anything but deserted. The oldest part of the park, it is also the section that has no duplicate anywhere. A combination of actual buildings moved in from the desert, restorations, and reconstructions — fitted out with antique vehicles and nineteenth-century artifacts — it also features such rides as log cars in a flume (45 m.p.h.), a ride through the interior of a mine, one on a restored stagecoach, one on a beautifully-maintained narrow-gauge steam train. You can also pan for gold (everyone discovers some), wander through some old-time shops, and in general absorb some good-humored old-fashioned atmosphere.

Several sidelights are also worth seeking out. Two of them are classic old merry-go-rounds, complete with band organs. One is a reproduction of Independence Hall in Philadelphia — American history brought West.

Special events enliven the park from time to time, as does a full entertainment schedule; both are announced in newspapers. And as part of the berry-farm heritage, you can buy Knott's preserves (the aromas from their preparation sometimes drifts across the park), and you can buy a cookbook of "theme" recipes.

LION COUNTRY SAFARI, Moulton Parkway at San Diego Freeway, Irvine (714) 837-1200.

The third park is the largest in size (500 acres), but requires probably no more than half a day to see. Still, it's unique: an expansive zoo where you're the captive (in your car) and the animals roam loose (if not free).

You can expect to see the animals up close, so you had better keep your car windows rolled up. The drive-through area comes in several sections, separated by concealed moats and fences, for this is not Africa — where animals mix together. Though the staging is much closer to nature than at a conventional zoo, there are still not enough animals or space for the natural food-chain situation where some eat others. Thus the lions and cheetahs are in their own compounds, while ostriches, graceful antelopes, elephants, towering giraffes, hippos, flamingos, and other creatures occupy premises with more mixed populations.

The best time to go is early morning or late afternoon, or even on cold or rainy days — for it is at such times that the animals are most active. As in Africa, they tend to get drowsy by mid-morning on warm days, and they may stay that way until at least mid-afternoon.

You may tarry along the road as long as you like to watch the animals. Then at the end of the drive-through area is a pedestrian section where birds and animals are to be seen in more conventional settings — some of them beside the course of a "river" boat ride. There you'll also find visitor diversions (shows, train ride, pedal boats) and eating places.

THE MUSEUMS AND THE SIDE SHOWS

Five museums or museum-like displays round out the collection of visitor attractions. Three have some connection with the film world, two emphasize automobiles, one is devoted to aircraft, and one — here almost by accident — is simply a curiosity.

MOVIELAND WAX MUSEUM and Palace of Living Art, 7711 Beach Boulevard, Buena Park (714) 522-1154

It's not just the 240 figures, it's the costumes and the nearly 100 film sets that make this more a kind of high temple of movie glory than a mere wax museum. The faces are mostly familiar, from early Chaplin to current TV luminaries, and a good many of them are startlingly convincing.

The display is flash carried to the flashpoint, and for its genre it's first class — surprisingly enough, considering the inherent potential for schlock. It is stunning with such devices as mirrored walls that project your reflected image in among the walk-past sets. Or with sets that you move through — such as the upside down engine room of *Poseidon,* right out of the film. It also includes original props from films (including cars), theatrical lighting, sound, special effects, and even such animation as one of the non-dead opening a coffin in the Bela Lugosi - Dracula set.

This is not a ride park, yet its variety is such that people often spend two hours or more here and at the adjacent living art display — a slight misnomer in that the "living" actually refers to wax reproductions of art masterworks shown in three-dimensional settings, along with the pieces after which they were modeled. The paintings are in the form of reproductions and the sculpture in the form of painstaking copies in Carrara marble — the most remarkable of which are Michelangelo's *Pieta,* inside, and *David,* outside.

There are also eating places along the way and outdoors in a new patio, and even a place where you can have a quick picture taken of yourself in the company of the likes of Frankenstein's monster.

BRIGGS CUNNINGHAM AUTOMOTIVE MUSEUM, 250 East Baker Street (at Red Hill Road), Costa Mesa (714) 546-7660

A shrine for the knowing aficionado of cars, this is one of the world's great collections for uniformly high quality. It has more than a hundred cars notable for their contributions, pacesetters that have established industry standards for technology, performance, and esthetics. All are beautifully restored, maintained, and operable. The outstanding car is a Bugatti Royale, one of only six ever built and possibly one of the ten most valuable cars in the world. Another is a 1927 Grand Prix Delage, never defeated on the racing circuit and winner of all four races it entered after returning from nine years of retirement. And there are five cars built and raced by owner Briggs Cunningham himself.

Recent acquisitions include a Frontenac racing car (1928-29), a supercharged Duesenberg racing car (1929-30), the first Ferrari in the United States (and one of the earliest known), and two Indianapolis racing cars of the present generation, on long-term loan.

MOVIELAND OF THE AIR — Tallman Aviation, Orange County Airport, Costa Mesa (714) 545-1193

The Cunningham car museum is west of the airport; this plane collection is east of it, or rather on the east side. It occupies hangars and outdoor space adjoining the runway south of the terminal on Campus Drive. Thirty to thirty-five planes are on display (the number varies as planes come and go; part of the business is providing aircraft for use in films). Most of the planes are in excellent condition, flyable, and a good many have been seen in films and on television. The emphasis is on World War I and II, with such rarities as a Curtiss Pusher, Boeing P-12, Jenny, Sopwith Camel, two B-25's and even a Grumman Duck J2F6.

MOVIE WORLD, 6920 Orangethorpe Avenue (at Knott Avenue), Buena Park (714) 523-1520

Cars permeate the miscellany in this gargantuan attic of a museum: celebrity and film-star cars (the psychedelic Bentley of the Beatles, the Horch car Hitler gave to Eva Braun), antique cars, movie cars (from *The Great Race,* for example), custom cars (Big Daddy Roth's Druid Princess and Rat Fink), and cut-away cars for filming. Interspersed with these are clusters of movie props, models, sets, and special-effects mechanisms, along with such participatory experiences as a maze to wander through and a great tube to slide down inside of. And more. Amazing. It may not be a primary destination, but one thing's for sure: There's nothing else quite like it. And such special events as car auctions are worth going to see.

OTHER EXOTIC DIVERSIONS

Finally, should your schedule permit, a little exploration of Orange County turns up a whole world of diverting commercial fun.

It is tempting to ascribe some of it to crazy California, but like many such novelties as miniature golf and go-carts, these may be just prototypes on their way to currency elsewhere.

Two are skateboard parks, where you can watch the kids in remarkable evolutions on silent wheels through abstract-sculpture geometry called "runs": Skatopia, at 7100 Knott Avenue, Buena Park (994-5060); and The Concrete Wave, 950 South Citron Street, Anaheim (991-6750).

These by no means make other skating obsolete. Indeed, both roller and ice skating (an exotic sport in this warm climate) thrive, with a dozen rinks around Orange County.

One auto-oriented establishment is part of the Malibu franchise chain, in which you drive a scaled-down race car on a scaled-down track, while you are clocked at equivalent speeds of full-sized cars: Malibu Grand Prix, at 2430 East Katella Avenue, Anaheim (634-0303).

Nor are go-carts obsolete. Probably the largest operation is Kartopia, 1062 Laguna Road, Tustin (836-0642).

The never-never land surroundings of miniature golf somehow seem related to all this, and that sport flourishes amain, with ten courses in the county. One is so large and elaborate it offers 90 holes.

And finally, there is The Wild Wild Wet, 888 South West Street, Anaheim (776-4680). Here the gambit is flume rides — only it's you, not a log car, that the falling water moves down the flume at high speed to a splash finish at the bottom.

Christian Brothers St. Helena winery was once largest in the world

Chapter 10:

Wine Country

NAPA VALLEY IS NOT a vacation place for families with kiddies. And on heavy weekends at season-height (harvest time, September into October), it may not even be for crowd-shy adults any more. Half a million people a year come to tour and taste.

Though just one of many wine districts in California, Napa Valley is still the *cor cordium,* the heart of hearts for those who worship at the altar of the noble grape. This heritage had long since taken root when Robert Louis Stevenson (late of the Monterey Peninsula) found "the stirring sunlight and the growing vines . . . a pleasant music for the mind," and ". . . the wine is bottled poetry."

Stevenson honeymooned in the mountains overlooking the valley in 1880, during the second glory era of wine-making. The first had been devoted to the hard-working but plebeian mission grape.

This second age was ushered in with the planting of more sophisticated European grapes in 1852 and the production of European-style wines by 1858. Then prosperity lasted until a depression in 1890, along with a dread disease that wiped out whole vineyards, crippled the industry. Prohibition in 1919 merely administered the *coup de grace.*

The third, today's Golden Age, began less than fifty years ago with the repeal of Prohibition in 1933. The rest is history: fifty wineries, twenty thousand acres of vineyards in a polyphasic climate as propitious for a wide variety of premium grapes as any on earth, producing some of the world's finest wines.

Much of today's crowd results from the valley's location just an hour from San Francisco. Thus it is a destination for travelers from more distant locations either by itself or as an extension of a San Francisco visit.

Contemporary Napa Valley is scenic not with dramatic landforms but with a kind of Old California rural charm, to which are added the two special ingredients of vineyards and wineries — many of which are antique and picturesque, some of which are new and picturesque.

The vineyards contribute color. There may be no other valley in California quite so exciting from late September through November, with its cloisonné-enamel patterns of intense yellows and reds, set off with splotches of green, orange and purple. This happens because grape leaves change to varying hues at different times according to variety and micro-climate of their location. Often the contrast is vivid just across a fence line between two fields — or even within one field of the same vines.

The other color show comes in January and February, in years of normal rainfall. Then, though the vines are still bare, new grass carpets the land between the vine rows with emerald, and the sunshine spill of yellow mustard flower creates an over-layer of color — all this in the "dead of winter."

For the motorist, the valley is a lopsided ladder. The more important leg is on the west side, running roughly north-northwest from the town of Napa. This is Highway 29, a *Route Du Vin* if ever any road merited the name in California, passing perhaps twenty wineries in thirty miles north from Napa — plus another dozen close off the highway.

Roughly parallel along the east side of the valley is the Silverado Trail — the stagecoach route of Stevenson's time, a century ago — today a route of lesser traffic and a third the number of wineries. Ten cross-valley roads link these two main roads like rungs of a ladder, and a scattering of wineries to be found along them, too. And finally, some roads lead out of the valley to the west, north, and east (this doesn't really spoil the ladder-in-the-valley image), passing another dozen or so wineries.

SEEING THE WINERIES AND THE TOWNS

The core of the Napa Valley vacation, of course, is visiting the wineries. There you learn how the wines are made and what subtle distinctions give them character. And there you taste the product — and buy, if you like.

Here are some of the major wineries along Highway 29 north of Napa that offer regular tours and tasting. Once their programs were free; now, with the increase in crowds some have begun to charge for admission and maybe tasting — though many do not.

Further along I set forth a sampling from half a hundred or so wineries, intended to offer the newcomer a variety of experiences. The assembling of a wine cellar I leave to your own further research. Happily there is plenty of help for this in the form of books and other publications — many of which also present more complete and detailed winery listings, along with telephone numbers and addresses of wineries where you must make an appointment for a tour.

One of the briefer listings is on a map published by the Napa County Development Council, a real help in getting around among so many wineries. Look for their visitor-information sign beside the highway in Napa.

When planning your day, consider the idea of a picnic. The picnic tradition got its start in the era when there were few places of quality to eat in the valley. Though that situation no longer applies, picnickers are still enthusiastic, for an alfresco meal can be a welcome counterpoint to the pleasures of the tasting room.

There is a distinct class of foods — including French or sourdough bread, cheeses, such sausages as salami, certain salad vegetables, and fresh fruits — with a real affinity for wine. These are readily available at dealers in picnic produce and provender along the way, noted in the text that follows.

A few wineries provide picnic tables for patrons. You will also find picnic facilities in city parks in St. Helena and Calistoga, and both Old Bale Mill and Bothe-Napa state parks in the valley. Or try an inviting setting beside one of the country roads across or out of the valley; non-litterers are not discouraged from such *fetes champetres*.

I omit Napa from the narrative as other than a starting point because it is slightly out of character as a relatively big place and not structured to accommodate the visitor. Still, there are a couple of motels and some restaurants, including two atmospheric ones: the Carriage House and the Victorian House.

The first winery is off the highway.

CHRISTIAN BROTHERS, MONT LA SALLE. On Redwood Road, about six miles west of Highway 29, this is one of two operated by the Christian Brothers, perhaps the largest producers in the valley. It has an extraordinarily photogenic setting, with its 1903 stone winery, novitiate school, and chapel dominating two hundred acres of vineyards.

YOUNTVILLE, at the end of the freeway that spoils the rural illusion in the lower part of the valley, is the first of a series of rather picturesque small towns.

Named for a Napa Valley pioneer, it is the site of Vintage 1870 — an erstwhile dilapidated winery of that date that now houses specialty shops in great variety, restaurants, and a theater — all in settings of vigilantly tasteful restoration-chic. Here you can take a champagne or champagne and brunch flight in a bright-colored hot-air balloon (when the wind is still or gentle). Call 944-8688 for a reservation.

Yountville is also the site of two restored lodging houses (see "Finding a Place to Stay" below), and of such culinary emporia as the Court of Two Sisters pastry shop, a juicery in a railroad car, a saloon-restaurant in a former livery stable and others. Quaintsville.

DOMAINE CHANDON. West of Yountville a short distance, this big but low-profile, barrel-vault-roof, 1977 winery is one of three in the valley primarily devoted to champagne (or "sparkling wine" if you make the French distinction that only wine from the Champagne district can bear that name). You may inspect a display of wine tools and presses from Champagne, tour the winery, and have lunch or dinner in the adjacent small but superior restaurant — where Chandon wines are served.

OAKVILLE, the next town name on the map to the north, is better described as a small settlement. It is the location (interpreting its limits liberally) of two picnic-food places that sell over the counter, Valley Cheese Co. and Oakville Grocery.

ROBERT MONDAVI WINERY. One of the dramatic newer ones, just north of Oakville, it has a highly visible building with an arch entrance to a courtyard and a simple tower. This is the scene of popular-music concerts in the summer — with wine-tasting at intermission — and art shows, a winter film festival, wine classes, and even cooking school courses at other times of the year.

Then comes Rutherford, likewise a minute place, possessor of a charming 1888 one-room schoolhouse as well as the Rutherford Square complex. This includes a soup-and-sandwich restaurant, ice cream shop, delicatessen, and a bar.

INGLENOOK VINEYARDS. An imposing, vine-covered landmark west of Rutherford, it dates its career from 1880 though the big winery and cellar was built in 1887. One of the valley's older wineries, it also has new construction that makes it one of the largest. The tasting room, an antique gem, is worth the visit for a look — quite apart from the quality of the wines.

BEAULIEU VINEYARD. Just north of Oakville, this is another first-class operation of respectable age (established 1900). It achieved fame for the work of its former winemaker, Andre Tchelistcheff, over a period of decades. Expanded in recent years under new ownership, the winery now has a visitor center with gardens, tasting room, and a theater for films on wine and the winemaking process.

V. SATTUI WINERY. About midway between Rutherford and St. Helena, this one dates back more than a century, though its present form represents a revival in 1975. A small family enterprise, it offers an informal kind of tour followed by tasting hosted by Daryl Sattui, and a cheese and gift shop where you can assemble the ingredients for a picnic under the trees outside.

HEITZ WINE CELLARS. A couple of miles south of St. Helena, this is a tasting and sales room only these days, although housed in the original winery from 1961. The present winery is almost directly east in Spring Valley.

LOUIS M. MARTINI WINERY. The third in a row east of Highway 29 and south of St. Helena, this prestigious winery dates from 1933 — when Prohibition was repealed — and is a large operation in volume, variety, and quality, with a reputation sustained over many years.

ST. HELENA, heart of the wine country, still projects an engaging sense of not having left the Victorian era quite behind. This is visible both in its brief downtown, where some splendid ornate buildings are beautifully cared for, and in its similarly compact residential area, where Victorian gems are shaded by long-since mature trees.

It is the home of some fascinating side aspects of the wine country. One is the Napa Valley Wine Library Association (housed in the city's public library at Oak and Adams

Streets), noted for its summer wine appreciation course — for which the waiting list is now lengthy indeed. Another, the Silverado Museum, houses the only substantial reminders of the sojourn of the valley's leading nineteenth-century publicist, Robert Louis Stevenson. The museum shares a great old Napa-style stone building at 1347 Railroad Avenue, a block east of Main Street, with the Hatchery — an art center. The third is an outlet for a locally pressed allied Mediterranean-climate product, olive oil — along with a complete, Italian-influenced delicatessen: the Napa Valley Olive Oil factory.

Two other places with picnic comestibles include W. F. Giugni and Son (also prepared foods) and Vintage Produce Center. Of several restaurants in town, La Belle Hélene is among the smallest, but maybe the most noted.

Then just north of town are two historic-landmark wineries.

BERINGER VINEYARD. This is one of the most atmospheric and best-kept of the wineries. The showplace of this 1876 establishment is the restored, exquisitely detailed Rhine House, a seventeen-room reproduction of the Beringer family estate in the Old Country — today used as a reception center. The tour begins with a film, and its highlight is the network of cool tunnels dug by Chinese labor into limestone hills behind the old three-story stone winery.

CHARLES KRUG WINERY. The oldest operating winery in Napa Valley, it dates from 1861, though expansion took place after 1933 and much modernization has occurred since then. There are tours and tastings, and on Saturday nights in August the chamber-musicales known as August Moon Concerts out under the oaks.

CHRISTIAN BROTHERS WINERY, GREYSTONE CELLARS. This monumental 1889 stone edifice just across the road from Krug was once the largest winery in the world. Owned by the Christian Brothers for half a century, it contains aging cellars and Charmat-process Champagne works, so tours are unusual for content as well as for scale. And there are tasting facilities.

FREEMARK ABBEY WINERY. Two miles north of St. Helena, this 1967-revival winery is housed in an 1895 stone building, and is nearly as notable for the company it keeps

Sterling winery occupies a commanding site at upper end of Napa Valley

as for its wines (not yet made in sufficient volume for tasting). The winery occupies the lower floor, while the upper floor contains The Abbey Restaurant, a gift and gourmet shop offering prepared foods as well as deli items, and the Hurd beeswax candle factory. This comes together as one of the great tourist stops of the valley.

Nearby on Lodi Lane you can observe coopers making barrels in the traditional way — along with currently-popular hot tubs.

Then so unobtrusively signed you can easily drive right by, Old Bale Mill State Historic Park adjoins the west side of the highway about three miles north of St. Helena. Setting for an excellent restoration of a marvelous old wooden waterwheel mill, named for its builder, it is well worth a stop for a look, a photograph, a picnic.

Just to the north of that is the much larger Bothe-Napa State Park, a big chunk of forest, including second-growth redwood, that offers picnicking, camping, hiking, and swimming in a pool.

HANNS KORNELL CHAMPAGNE CELLARS. On Larkmead Road, east of Highway 29, it is one of two superlative champagne wineries hereabouts. It has tours, followed by tasting, whenever enough visitors gather.

SCHRAMSBERG VINEYARDS. Also a champagne specialist, this is the valley's third historic-landmark winery. Five miles north of St. Helena, it dates from 1862 and is the second oldest — or the oldest of the hillside wineries. It was notable enough in Stevenson's time to be included in his book, *Silverado Squatters*. Today, you must call ahead for an appointment to look at the wine-making process. Volume is too small to permit tasting, but this is one of the few places where you can buy such of the wines as are available.

STERLING VINEYARDS. On Dunaweal Lane, east of Highway 29, this stunning white Greek-isle evocation is worth the visit for its view alone, on a mini-mountain overlooking a spectacular panorama of vineyard-covered valley bottom. One of the few wineries to be designed (in 1968) for visitors, it is laid out for self-guided tours and it has a tasting room and a picnic area. You reach it via an aerial tramway (for which there is a charge).

CALISTOGA is the valley's northernmost town. A mixture of funky old and market-town modern, it is liberally sprinkled with spas from an early day when it aspired to resort status. For some of the story, drop in on the Napa County Historical Society Museum.

Apart from a good Mexican restaurant, the eating has tended more to the down-home than the epicurean, though a new restaurant in the newly-remodeled train depot promises some variety.

There are some unusual diversions. One is sailplaning in silent grace over the valley, with airplane-towed takeoff from the airport close in (call 942-5592 for information, or stop by). And one of the hot springs places has swimming for the public. Other things in the vicinity are more purely tourist: a miniature train ride on Silverado Trail just south of town, and the geysers and petrified forest northwest and west of town.

FINDING A PLACE TO STAY

The wineries are clearly the goal, but what about a place to stay?

There aren't as many as you might expect, possibly because traffic is too seasonal, but there are some interesting ones. Whichever you choose, reserve several weeks or a month in advance during summer and fall. You can get a list of accommodations from the Napa County Development Council, P.O. Box 876, Napa 94558 (or 1900 Jefferson Street).

Two that I find especially interesting are the restored stone Napa Valley-style Burgundy House Inn and Magnolia Hotel in Yountville, both small, both full of atmosphere. Another old-timer is Chalet Bernensis, a great old Victorian house revived with five guest rooms. It is on Highway 29 just south of St. Helena — with Sutter Home Winery next door and Louis Martini across the road.

Some unusual places are on the edge or outside the valley. One of these is Silverado Country Club, an oak-studded 1,200-acre estate now a condominium development operated as a resort, east of Napa. You stay in an apartment and eat there or at a grill or in the dining room of an 1870 mansion. You play on two 18-hole golf courses or eight tennis courts, swim in any of five pools, ride a bicycle. Nearby are horseback riding and hiking.

Somewhat unorthodox (and maybe more a destination for lunch or dinner) is Pope Valley Parachute Ranch, for devotees of sky diving. It is on Pope Valley Road about 12 miles from Napa Valley (take Deer Park Road east; it becomes Howell, then Mountain Road before intersecting Pope Valley Road). You can take lessons, rent equipment, or just watch — or stay for a meal at the simple Lodge there.

Up in Calistoga are the spas that survive from that town's 1860 origins as a hot-spring resort: Dr. Wilkinson's and Golden Haven are two of eight that offer accommodations of varying degrees of venerableness, along with massage, hot baths, and other treatments. Calistoga Spa has two hot-water pools open to the public, one outdoors, one covered.

SIDE TRIP: SONOMA, *Valley of the Moon*

Reigning Napa Valley has a challenger in neighboring Sonoma Valley on two counts: scenery and longevity in the wine industry. Sonoma also has physical evidence of its own literary light, Jack London, and a historic shrine: Sonoma Town, one of the richer living-history spots in California.

A pleasant country road approaches the London place from Napa Valley. From Oakville, head southwest into the mountains on Oakville Grade (it becomes Dry Creek, then Trinity Road) to Glen Ellen, and follow signs to Jack London State Historic Park. This preserves the burnt remains of the colorful novelist's Wolf House and the 1919 house his wife built after his death — full of memorabilia. His grave is nearby.

Then take Highway 12 down the valley to Sonoma, a town of one square mile at the time of founding. It was laid out around a Mexican-style central plaza — today a large park of lawn and trees in the middle of which is set a determinedly Yankee-period city hall.

Most of the interest is arrayed around the west, north, and east sides of the plaza. On First Street West (one of two First Streets at either end of the plaza), you encounter the old Union Hotel and Hall. Then comes the 1836-46 Salvador Vallejo house (he was the brother of the estimable Spanish-Mexican-American General Mariano Vallejo, who founded the town in 1835). Both places are historic landmarks.

On Spain Street, the north side of the plaza, are: the 1850 Swiss Hotel (built by Salvador, now a restaurant), Casa Grande (Mariano's first house, of which a remaining wing is now a museum), and the massive 1836 Sonoma Barracks. In process of restoration, it was also built by General Vallejo.

At the northeast corner is a restored 1840 remnant of Mission San Francisco Solano, northernmost and last (1823) of the California missions. Now a museum, it displays an impressive collection of mission paintings. This is one of the parts of Sonoma State Historic Park; keep your admission ticket to get into the Vallejo place, described below.

Also at this corner are a monument to the short-lived, almost comic-opera Bear Flag revolt, which preceded the American conquest in 1846. And the 1840 Blue Wing Inn, another of the industrious general's constructions.

Filling out the spaces around the plaza are a number of stores, some in Victorian-era buildings — including a cheese factory, a French bakery, an old-fashioned ice cream shop.

Old buildings (and antique shops) continue for a block or so east on both Napa and Spain streets. On Fourth Street East, beyond, and half a block north of Spain, is the Sebastiani Winery. They own Sonoma's first vineyard, planted in 1825. You may tour the winery, taste the wines, and see an Indian artifact collection.

Take Napa east to Winery Road, then turn left to its end, to find one of the region's most colorful stone wineries: Buena Vista. First of the post-mission-era wineries, it was founded by Count Agoston Haraszthy in 1857. Now restored and a historic landmark, it has a tasting room in a cool tunnel and a shaded picnic area for patrons.

Then from the plaza once more, take Spain Street west two blocks and go north on Third to see General Vallejo's 1850 two-story adobe Victorian house, *Lachryma Montis* ("Tears of the Mountain," named for a spring on the estate). Also part of the state historic park, it has a museum collection and a rural setting to enjoy.

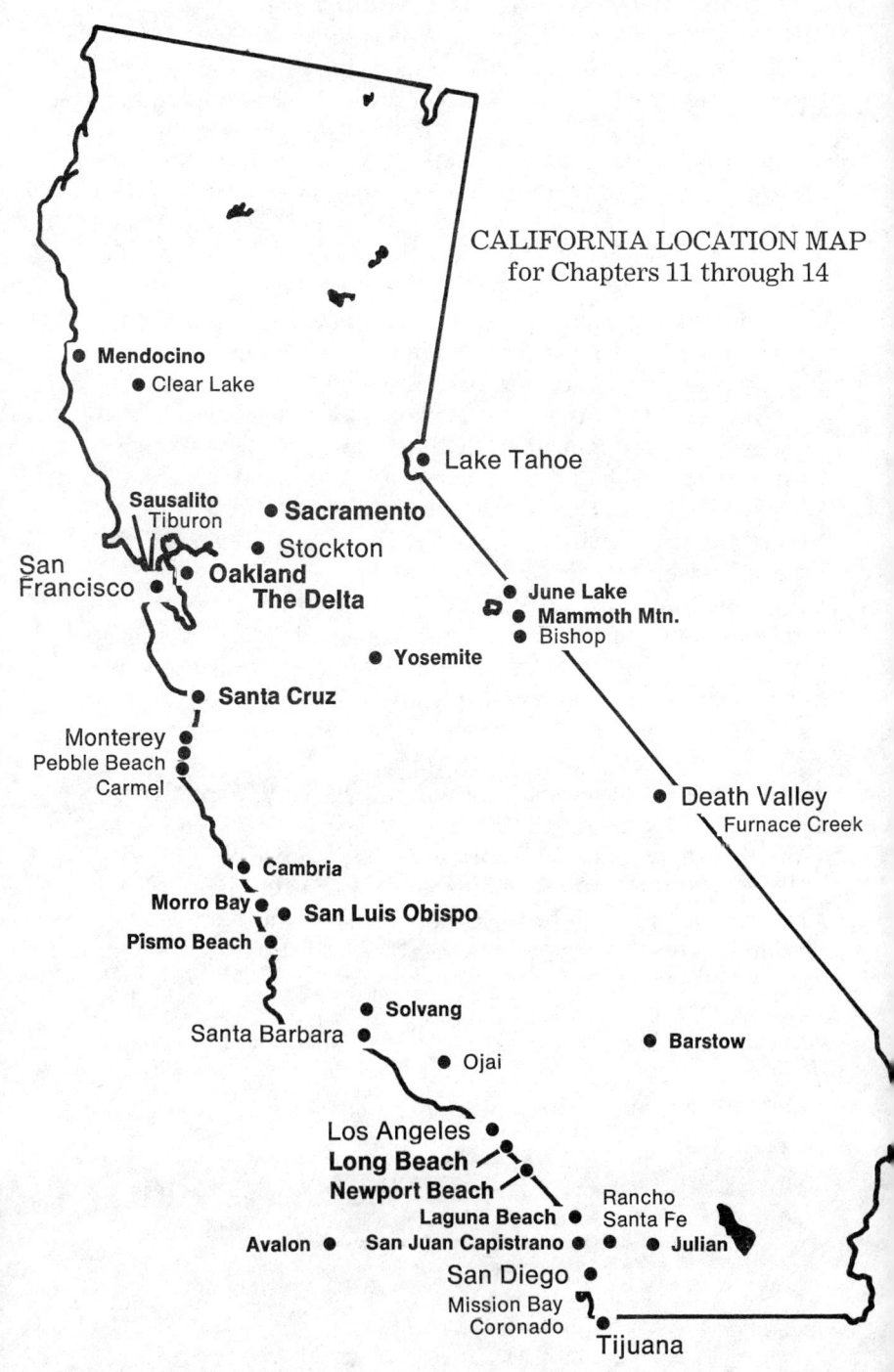

Chapter 11:

Top 10 Resorts

B Y RESORT I MEAN a place where you can stay awhile that has facilities for recreation. The nominations here are based on such self-sufficiency, all-year season, and general merit.

One dates back to the 1880's, when California was a winter resort place and trains brought fashionable Easterners for "the season." Half of them date from the 1920's — another great resort period — their survival a testimony to continuing excellence. The remainder, from after World War II, achieved quality despite newness.

Descriptions in this chapter are intended to help you select the style of resort that appeals to you. Principal recreations are listed, including golf and tennis when they are conveniently close, even if not physically on the premises.

I have not gone into rates, which are both complex (varying with season and type of accommodation) and changeable. When you ask about them, ask also about package plans, for they are potential bargains and they can give you an idea how much your holiday will cost altogether.

Many package rates imply off-peak reductions for season and even days of the week. Remember, Californians can enjoy some splendid seasonal weather that refugees from snowy climes overlook — the period just after Labor Day being notable.

In comparing rates, make sure you do not compare American Plan ("AP", all meals included) with Modified American Plan 'MAP", some meals included) or European Plan ("EP", you're on your own for meals).

Also find out about charges for use of facilities. Some might be free, but if not, charges for golf, tennis courts, and horses can add up rapidly. Some package plans, for golfers and tennis players, for example, may include such items.

Note also that most places charge room tax (seldom mentioned in the literature) and some also add a service charge in place of individual tips.

Finally — in these days of energy shortage — if you plan to go by public transportation, ask about transfer to the resort: how, and how much it costs. There are some surprises, such as a small-plane service from Bay Area airports to Clear Lake.

THE ALISAL
P.O. Box 26, Solvang, California 93463 (805) 688-6411
MAP Horse activities, Golf, Tennis, Swimming, Fishing, Boating

Alisal (Spanish for "Sycamore Grove") may be the best resort left in California for horse persons. But while it offers a full range of lessons, rides on more than fifty trails, alfresco breakfasts, picnics, and steak fries, plus hay rides and ring events, it is by no means single-mindedly horsey.

A 10,000-acre working ranch on a Spanish land grant, set among serene, oak-studded hills near Solvang, it has space enough to accommodate golf, tennis, and a swimming pool. And it has a small lake for summer use, where kids can go swimming, fishing, and boating (and so can adults). Summer, in fact, is for families with kids, and a comprehensive day-camp program is offered.

You stay in one of sixty cottage rooms under the trees, and eat at your choice of American-plan dining room or a public dining room (where there is evening entertainment three or four nights a week all year) — or lunch at the golf clubhouse or beside the pool in summer. There are no telephones or television sets in the rooms — absences for which most guests are soon grateful — but they are available in public rooms.

FURNACE CREEK INN AND RANCH RESORT
Death Valley, California 92328 (800) 622-0838
AP (Inn), EP (Ranch) Tennis (Inn guests only), Swimming, Horse and mule riding, Golf, Bicycling

Centrally located at sea level on the eastern edge of the vast salt flats of Death Valley, the Inn is positioned for a view, while the Ranch nestles close by below in a date palm grove amid irrigated lawns. Together they comprise the major settlement in the valley.

Stay at the Inn if you like the elegant, old-line kind of resort, with a dress-up dining room or a more casual supper club (with entertainment), tennis courts, and swimming pool. The 70-room adobe building dates from 1927 and is handsomely furnished and air-conditioned. The Inn is open November through April.

Stay at the Ranch for a more informal atmosphere (and a more modest price) in a motel room — the number was recently expanded to 225 — air-conditioned and open all year. Besides its own swimming pool, the Ranch has the golf course, riding horses and mules, and rental bicycles for both Inn and Ranch guests. It also has a notable museum of the borax mining days, along with an outdoor collection of historic vehicles from carriages to a steam locomotive. You can eat in a cafeteria (where evening movies are sometimes shown) coffee shop, or steak house, and there is a cocktail lounge. A store, laundry, post office, and gas station round out the facilities.

Nearby is Death Valley National Monument headquarters, with its museum of history and natural history, and information on roads, trails, and tours.

HOTEL DEL CORONADO
Coronado, California 92118 (714) 435-6611
EP Swimming, Tennis, Health spa, Bicycling, Golf, Boating

The first ninety years have been kind to this splendid Victorian resort hotel, among the last of the great wooden pleasure palaces left in America. There is a 200-room modern annex if you absolutely insist on newness, but the 400 rooms in the old building have the charm of their era (though modern facilities have been added).

The awesome room is the main dining hall, with its soaring wooden ceiling like a ship inverted, but the towers, lobby, carved-wood bars, antique brasswork elevator, grand ballroom, and a hundred details of the craftsmanship of yesteryear contribute to the delight. Take the Saturday afternoon guided tour for an eyeful and earful of colorful history and curious superlatives.

The major amenity is the seashore. This is the only really big hotel right on an ocean beach on the Pacific Coast. Other facilities on the 33-acre premises include an enormous swimming pool, tennis courts, and a health complex. And not far away in town are golf, boats for charter or rental, bikeways — and even lawn bowling greens.

THE INN AT RANCHO SANTA FE
P.O. Box 869, Rancho Santa Fe, CA. 92067 (714) 756-1131
EP Tennis, Swimming, Golf, Horseback riding, Bicycling

Even though San Diego County should fill with subdivisions, Rancho Santa Fe — in a former Santa Fe Railroad eucalyptus tree plantation — will remain a forested island of the country-estate good life, spread out around its charming little 1920's town center. And its Inn, adjoining that center, will remain a genteel retreat.

Set among trees that date from its founding in 1924, and located not far north of the city and several miles in from the sea, it offers the lure of the quiet hideaway. The action is tennis on the grounds, or lolling by the swimming pool, or a round of golf at any one of three excellent courses nearby, or a horseback ride across a rural landscape, or a bicycle ride on a country road. In the summer, guests can also use a beach house in nearby Del Mar, adding the option of surf and sand.

The 75 rooms, in the original building or in cottages in the garden, have individuality — most with sitting room space, some with kitchens or refrigerators. Lunch and dinner may be served indoors or out on a terrace next to the dining room. And in summer there is music for dancing Friday and Saturday nights.

KONOCTI HARBOR INN
8727 Soda Bay Road, Kelseyville, CA. 95451 (707) 279-4281
EP Swimming, Boating, Fishing, Water skiing, Tennis, Golf

This one is a sleeper, a little-known playtime village of 250 guest rooms and apartments, plus a recreation complex that includes a marina, two large swimming pools (and two small ones for children), dining, coffee shop, and entertainment spaces, and even a grocery store. All this fills 129 acres, pleasantly landscaped, that slope down to the shore of big Clear Lake, about 1½ hours north of San Francisco by car.

There are plenty of shore activities: tennis, miniature golf (and full-sized golf not far away), and baseball, playground, and teen center for the youngsters.

But the major emphasis is the water. You can launch your own boat, or moor it here, or rent a boat (small to cabin-cruiser size) for fishing, or just an excursion, or even water skiing. Boat and tackle are available, and you can take ski lessons in the summer. There are also trips on the Inn's big paddlewheeler. The place is liveliest in the summer, and that is when there are the most things for kids to do.

THE LODGE AT PEBBLE BEACH
Pebble Beach, California 93953 (408) 624-3811
EP or MAP, Golf, Tennis, Handball, Health spa, Swimming, Horseback riding, Hiking

Formerly known as Del Monte Lodge, this is one of those places that has built up an unassailable mystique over the years (since 1919) — a mystique that has much to do with the magic of its romantic setting in the Del Monte Forest (Monterey pine and cypress) beside a rocky seacoast.

The setting has attracted world fame for its golf courses and tournaments and for the celebrities who have played there. The courses — three championship and one nine-hole, par-three — are superb. There are also tennis, swimming, handball, and sauna facilities. And there are horses for riding trails in the forest, plus non-bridle trails for hikers and joggers.

You stay in a spacious room in the main lodge or in one of ten separate buildings; there are 135 rooms. The lodge has a splendid old-style "living room" with a big fireplace, easy chairs, and what has to be one of the world's most engaging views: lawn and pines (the eighteenth green of the Pebble Beach Golf Course) and rocks and kelp beds in the sea. And the food is superior, either in the dining room or in the continental restaurant in the lodge. There is entertainment most nights.

MARRIOTT'S SANTA BARBARA BILTMORE
1260 Channel Dr., Santa Barbara, CA. 93108 (805) 969-2261
EP or MAP Swimming, Tennis, Golf, Bicycling, Horseback riding, Fishing

"The Biltmore" has for more than half a century been the elegant beach hotel par excellence — one of few hostelries in California actually on the seashore. Set in nearly 23 acres of garden, it is a Mediterranean-style complex that offers a sense of refuge from a less ordered world outside.

There is a swimming pool on the grounds, an adjacent

club — to which guests are admitted — with a huge high-buoyancy pool (half salt water), and there are golf, tennis, and horses for riding not far away. Guests may go fishing from a pier on the beach in front of the hotel or go to sea in boats (fishing and sightseeing) out of Santa Barbara's harbor. And the hotel has bicycles for guests to ride on the shady streets of Montecito all around.

The dining rooms are among Santa Barbara's notable eating places, and the entertainment every night but Monday is attended by locals as well as guests. The 178 rooms and suites are situated in the main building and in garden cottages.

OJAI VALLEY INN
Ojai, California 93023 (805) 646-5511
AP Golf, Tennis, Swimming, Horseback riding, Bicycling

If you like country club atmosphere, try this resort in a picturesque mountain valley setting, at 1,000 feet of elevation, with an all-year climate (though warm on summer days). It is located about 1½ hours up the coast from Los Angeles and inland from Ventura, just outside the town of Ojai (say "OH-high").

Besides the golf (and an 18-hole putting green), there are tennis courts, a big swimming pool, and a stable with horses for rides on the expansive grounds and on many miles of trail beyond. Bicycles are also available for back-road riding. In the summer, the Inn stages barbecues and other meals outdoors in a country setting, and square dances on Saturday nights.

You stay in one of 110 rooms either in the 1923 original inn building or in other units added later — many with terrace or patio. There are three dining rooms, and entertainment on Friday and Saturday nights. Meals and cocktails are served out-of-doors during benign weather.

QUAIL LODGE
8205 Valley Greens Drive, Carmel, CA. 93921 (408) 624-1581
EP Golf, Tennis, Swimming, Bicycling

Quail Lodge is a successful essay in quality of environment without opulence or stiffness. Quality infuses the furnishings and fabrics of the 96 rooms, the architecture, and the landscape itself — a 245-acre plantation of trees and golf greenery, dotted with so many lakes that not only resident but migratory ducks and geese come flocking.

It is a golf and tennis resort, with swimming and bicycling through its suburban (or perhaps exurban) setting in gentle Carmel Valley.

And it's an outpost of good living. You stay in a cottage room, have breakfast and lunch at the golf clubhouse down the road, and dinner in the Covey — a handsome restaurant overlooking a night-lit water-course enlivened by waterfowl.

The quaint charm of the village of Carmel, the picturesque antiquities of Monterey, the forests of Monterey Peninsula, and such gems as Carmel Mission and Point Lobos State Reserve are all nearby.

VACATION VILLAGE HOTEL
P.O. Box 9509, San Diego, California 92109 (714) 274-4630
EP Golf, Tennis, Swimming, Bicycles, Boating, Fishing

This is really a pleasure village, in a 43-acre garden on an island (reached by bridge) in Mission Bay, the great aquatic park in San Diego. The garden is laced with water features — ponds and finger lagoons and four swimming pools. And set amid the trees, shrubs, and flowers are cottages with 340 rooms (including a palatial Presidential Suite). Some rooms open right onto the beach, others inland — but with a water garden prospect.

The beach and bay are the main event, with surfless swimming and boats and water skiers (you can rent a sailboat or paddleboat at the hotel dock). On shore there are tennis courts, bicycles for rent, a small golf course on the grounds and a big one close by — lit for night play. You can go fishing on the beach, or join a party boat for ocean fishing in Mission Bay.

And you can enjoy the buildings for their whimsy as well as their use: the focal-point view tower like a Steinberg ink drawing made three-dimensional, curved-roof pavilions, one of which holds the coffee shop, the underground Barefoot Bar for the casually inclined. Or, you can admire buildings for their distinction as well, such as the handsome one that houses dining and meeting rooms and the bar where evening entertainment takes place.

Casino is a 1920's landmark overlooking boats anchored in Avalon Harbor

Chapter 12:

Top 10 Seaside Towns

ONE OF THE PLEASANTEST vacations my wife and I ever took had simple ground rules: keep to the coast, stay in any engaging beach town we happened into, and move on to the next when the spirit so moved. The aim was that unique relaxation that only the edge of the sea can induce — whether you are sunning on the sand, or walking a rocky shore, or sniffing the sea tang of a port where great ships come and go.

So here I propose a similar movable adventure among some of the best towns oriented to the sea. It is easiest before Memorial Day or after Labor Day, when crowds thin out, but feasible in summer, too. The list is alphabetical, so it may as well start with an island:

AVALON

Tiny Avalon (population 1,800 in slightly more than a square mile), is the only island city offshore from mainland California.

Thousands of day visitors show up in summer and on holidays, many in their own boats, but the true island state of mind is reserved for those who stay over for a night or two. Accommodations are comfortable if not luxurious, and the one-time lack of good restaurants off-season has been rectified. The place projects a real sense of isolation — away from, if not out of sight of, the world dimly seen on the horizon.

Avalon is compact enough to achieve some of the pedestrian-scale charm of towns in Mexico or on the Riviera, and its landscape is similar. Its pleasures are the quiet ones: a stroll along the beach or out on the pier, a bicycle ride, a boat trip offshore or a day of deep-sea fishing, a short open-air bus tour to the dramatic heights above town or a half-day trip into the early-California landscape of the island's interior, a walk or ride up Avalon Canyon to a garden of native and exotic plants. You can also do the conventional resort thing: golf, tennis, horseback riding, lazing beside a pool.

And the boat ride over from Long Beach or San Pedro is a sea adventure that sets a mood and sets Avalon apart from all other vacation places in California. So is the short (15-minute) plane ride from the Catalina Terminal in San Pedro or Long Beach Airport.

LA JOLLA *(See Chapter 1)*

LAGUNA BEACH

This once-remote settlement of artists and escapists has long since lost its isolation and become an expensive seaside suburb, but the charm of its rocky shore, cove beaches, clear waters for divers, sea bluffs, hillside houses, and crooked streets remains.

There are motels aplenty and more than a dozen restaurants of many persuasions. You can walk the picturesque bluff-tops in Heisler Park and enjoy Main Beach — Laguna's "window to the sea," edged by boardwalk and park. And you can explore the nicely revived central shop area on foot — while the commercial strip follows the coast highway for several miles. But a principal lure will always be the beach: the sand, the surf, the rocks, the ebb-tide pools, the flourishing kelp beds.

And so will the art tradition. The Laguna Beach Art Museum has a splendid collection of an under-recognized flowering of California art that took place the first third of this century. And art and crafts fairs in winter and summer attract crowds. The summer show includes the celebrated Pageant of the Masters (live tableaus of famous works of art), for which you must secure tickets well in advance.

LONG BEACH — LOS ANGELES HARBORS

This is the heavy action, the busiest deep-sea harbor on the coast. Its two parts are administratively separate, but for the visitor they seem a physical unit — protected from the sea by a long breakwater from Point Fermin almost to the San Gabriel River.

Long Beach is the more complex and has the better visitor facilities, including hotels — if you want to immerse in the seafaring scene for a day or two.

Starting at the Orange County line, you first encounter Alamitos Bay. This contains beach on the sea and bay sides, yacht clubs, marinas, a seawall shop and restaurant complex (where you can get on an excursion boat for a trip around the bay), channels and residential canals, and the Marine Stadium — a water-course where you can sometimes watch crew and powerboat races.

Westerly from there is a long reach of nearly waveless beach, interrupted by the Belmont Pier, where you can fish over the side or go out on a party boat. From there on the narrow Bluff Park edges the shore almost to downtown, burgeoning these days with new construction — including two theaters at the new convention center. To seaward here are an amusement park, an emerging complex of lagoons, boat-launching ramps, and the Catalina boat landing.

Just beyond the mouth of the Los Angeles River, and beyond a channel often busy with water skiers, are a new hotel, a restaurant, and the looming hulk of *Queen Mary* — with a neo-British shopping village alongside. The ship is a hotel, restaurant and shop aggregation, museum, and goal for tours.

From there on across Terminal Island you pass through a working port replete with bizarre constructions, mechanical monsters that move large cargoes in the new era of bulk and container shipping. There are also a sportfishing landing, piers from which cruise ships sail, and a naval shipyard — marked by the tallest crane on the coast, a German giant liberated two wars ago.

On the Los Angeles side but still on Terminal Island, the *Princess Louise* — a restaurant aboard a ship — moors on the Main Channel. Then beyond the soaring Vincent Thomas Bridge you encounter the Catalina Terminal (ships and amphibious planes), and then the restaurants and shops of the Ports O'Call-Whaler's Village development. Here you can ride a helicopter, ride to the top of a tall view spire, and take a party or a harbor cruise excursion.

Nearby are the picturesque commercial fishing docks, and around the corner is the Twenty-Second Street Landing, a marina and fishing party boat operation. Farther seaward, past the large Fort MacArthur reservation, you come to Cabrillo Beach. This city park has beaches on the harbor and sea sides of the breakwater, a fishing pier inside the breakwater, and the lively Cabrillo Marine Museum — noted for its public programs during the grunion and whale seasons.

Finally, your exploration should end with a trip up to the heights of Point Fermin, where there is a restored old lighthouse in a park and spectacular views over the harbor, south to the mountains of Orange County, and out to Catalina.

MENDOCINO

About as far from San Francisco as San Diego is from Los Angeles (125 miles), Mendocino is a former logging town and seaport that somehow has managed to keep its intimate size and wooden-sidewalk flavor, even after a boom threatened dramatic expansion. Citizens rallied in time, and now zoning protects the mixture of plain Old New England and fussy Victorian antiquity, while a state park (Mendocino Headlands) preserves the once-threatened blufftop meadow between the village and the sea.

Today, Mendocino no longer has the eight hotels and twenty-one saloons of its heyday more than a century ago, but there are restaurants, a restored hotel and inn for overnight stay, and some forty sometimes self-conscious arts, crafts, and other shops. It makes a quaint basing point for seeing a scenic stretch of the North Coast.

That stretch extends roughly from where State Highway 128 reaches the sea north to Fort Bragg — or to MacKerricher State Park, north of that. (Or it might extend slightly south to Elk, site of two old inns where you can stay; two more of them are located a little north of there at Little River.)

It's a windswept land of rugged cliffs, rocky shore and beach sand dunes, river mouth and cove and lagoon, and upland forest. It's a land of summer fog and winter rain, though benign sunny spells occur — chiefly in fall and spring.

Three state parks with campgrounds, often full in summer, set aside some of the best landscapes: Van Damme, Russian Gulch, and MacKerricher. The Mendocino Coast Botanical Gardens, about two miles south of Fort Bragg, show off in nearly fifty acres the glories of rhododendrons — many of them hybrids from the natives that bloom along here from April through early June. Azaleas, begonias, fuchsias, and other flowers also do well in this cool, moist climate.

Trolley line once ended at Balboa Pavilion, beside Newport Harbor

The little town of Noyo, in a long, protected cove, is a picturesque haven for a fleet of commercial and sportfishing vessels that huddle in the harbor when weather at sea is bad.

Fort Bragg is the metropolis of this stretch of coast, with its 5,000 people. It, too, is a fishing and lumber town — with some aspects of a company town, and at the mill there are a museum and guided tours. Fort Bragg is the seaward end of the popular Skunk rail trip. The Skunk is a gasoline-powered rail car, dating from 1925, that plies a scenic route across the forested coast range to Willits, on Highway 101. It runs all year, while steam and diesel-locomotive trains, both called "Super Skunk," run in summer and during heavy-visitor periods the rest of the year. Round trips take about six hours. You're on your own for amusement at either end; at Willits, look into the Far West and Mendocino County museums during the layover.

MORRO BAY

A line of nine volcanic peaks that marches west from San Luis Obispo to the sea ends in the isolated monolith of Morro Rock, landmark of Morro Bay — the town and the estuarine lagoon.

The town sits on the landward side of the bay, just inside an entrance dredged for a harbor. It is partly picturesque, partly not, but it has all the interest lent by the sea and by serious fishing activity: jetties, piers, collections of fishing boats (commercial and sportfishing), restaurants that emphasize seafood, and fish markets. And there is the Clam Taxi, a boat that will take you out to the sandspit that marks the seaward edge of the bay and pick you up later — allowing plenty of time for digging, shore fishing, or beachcombing over on the ocean side of that strip of dunes.

The sandspit is part of the town's great nearby amenity, Morro Bay State Park. The park is part natural, with an excellent nature museum overlooking the bay and offering a close view of birds that throng the tidal flats. Great blue herons frequent a rookery in tall trees close by. The park covers much of the shore of the estuary, one of the great productive ones left on the coast, and acts to preserve the natural scene.

The park is also partly recreation-oriented, with a campground, a small-boat harbor, and a golf course on the slopes of Black Hill — next to last in the chain of volcanic peaks.

NEWPORT BEACH

The city of Newport Beach extends from the cliffs of Corona del Mar inland to encompass the vast expanses of Upper Newport Bay — thronged with waterfowl, migrant and resident. And it extends westward to include the districts of Balboa, Newport Beach proper, and the harbor — home to one of the great concentrations of pleasure craft on the coast.

All this provides a wide choice of beach, from the sands of "big" and "little" Corona (parts of a state beach) east of the harbor jetty, to great stretches of sand on the seaward side of the peninsula that encloses the harbor (where the west jetty creates the famous monumental waves of "the Wedge") to tiny pockets of beach beside harbor channels, to the Newport Dunes concession area north of the coast highway (admission, boats for rent).

And there are some choice urban districts to walk: the Lido Village and Cannery Village areas, the vicinity of the Newport Pier (site of the famous Dory Fish Market on the beach), the section around the grand old Balboa Pavilion (boats for rent, boat excursions, fishing party boats, and the tiny ferry over to Balboa Island), and the mini-"downtown" of Balboa Island.

The main ingredients of the place's character are these beach and old resort areas. Some of the rest is less intimate, though often distinctive: shops and restaurants along the main artery of the coast highway, stores and a hotel in the big shopping center inland overlooking town, and the Newporter Inn overlooking the upper bay. There's plenty to explore, though you may need patience; there will be a number of other people doing the same thing.

PISMO BEACH

Pismo Beach — the town — has the funky sea-faded air of a one-time resort past its prime in the off-season, but an air of timelessness when crowds are there. It has a dozen motels and several restaurants, and you can fish there from the shore or on the pier, or go out on a party boat, and go clamming.

The Pismo clam is king: a succulent creature that occurs from San Francisco south into Baja California, but reaches its optimum along this piece of coast. Hardly a restaurant in town doesn't serve chowder, and most people in town know when the next low tide will take place. Low tide reveals the least picked-over clam beds; the daytime minus tides of winter do so most dramatically — and attract the heaviest crowds. Even then, increasingly the successful clammer wears a wet suit and wades or dives beyond the wave line. You can buy a fishing license and rent clamming gear in Pismo Beach and neighboring towns.

Pismo Beach — the beach — is the northern end of a strand that reaches majestically south, curving west beyond the Santa Maria River, forming a broadside to ocean waves and wind that causes sand to collect and dunes to form. Indeed, the Pismo-Nipomo-Santa Maria dunes are among the most impressive in California, an important recreational resource as well as an unusual plant-community environment. The area includes a clutch of dune-impounded fresh-water lakes south of Oceano and just west of Highway 1.

Pismo State Beach occupies more than six miles of coastline south of town. It has campgrounds and is favored by clammers, shore fishermen, and dune buggy enthusiasts (who swarm on the big holiday weekends). Ramps from road to beach allow access for car.

You can also swim, though you might prefer the warm-water haven of Avila State Beach, up the coast a few miles. It also has a launching ramp, fishing pier, and sportfishing boats.

SANTA BARBARA *(See Chapter 5)*

SANTA CRUZ

Happy plebeians never lost their primal joy in the great Boardwalk amusement center at Santa Cruz, while it took self-conscious sophisticates the whole space of the era of Victorian rediscovery to come round to appreciating it. The classical merry-go-round and roller coaster are gems, as is the grand old ballroom, and even its modern-day thrill rides are part of a cherished American tradition. And so are the immemorial trimmings: cotton candy and candied apples, and chocolate-covered bananas (said to be the culinary contribution of Newport Beach).

There is more to Santa Cruz as a beach-side town, of course. There's Natural Bridges State Beach a little way out, with its arches eroded into sandstone walls and its convocations of monarch butterflies in fall and spring. Then there's the noted West Cliff Drive closer in, leading to the central complex of the Municipal Wharf — with its anglers, bait shops, deep-sea party boats, fish markets, even sea lions — and the central beach, location of the Boardwalk.

Santa Cruz Small Craft Harbor, just beyond the San Lorenzo River holds the fishing fleet as well as pleasure craft. It is reached by East Cliff Drive, trickier to stay on and not as spectacular as its western counterpart. Together with Schwan Lake (a wildlife preserve), the harbor forms Twin Lakes State Beach, one of a series along Monterey Bay that includes New Brighton, Seacliff, and others.

Santa Cruz also has inland interest. The mission site includes a Spanish adobe, and though the mission is gone a half-scale replica is there. The Pacific Avenue Garden Mall, with its restored atmosphere, trees, and galleries, shops and restaurants, gives you a look at what Santa Barbara might have been like had not the 1925 earthquake destroyed its Victorian main street. The sign-posted 29-mile Tree-Sea Tour is a drive that goes inland past the university (the arrival of which may have had something to do with Santa Cruz's modern renaissance) through the redwoods to Felton (see the covered bridge, ride the narrow-gauge steam train) and Aptos. And of course, there are the side shows: the "gravity-defying" Mystery Spot, Santa's Village, and life-sized Last Supper figures in wax.

It's an old-time beach playland, gone respectable.

Windmill and shingles laid like thatch add to Solvang atmosphere

Chapter 13:

Top 10 Small Cities, Towns, and Hideaways

THIS GROUPING, I confess, is a miscellany. And its components are by no means ranked in order of superiority. I include it as an idea list for when you want something different to do on a weekend or some unusual place to go.

The hideaway motif runs through the collection, as does the motif of smallness for its own sake. (Note some overlap here with Chapter 12. For example, towns like Avalon could also qualify here for mini-scale and even hideaway quality.) The third idea is places most people overlook: Oakland, Sacramento, even Barstow. Don't expect the full measure of visitor services in some of them; do expect the fun of discovery.

BARSTOW, *Hub of the High Desert*

Barstow gets my nomination here not for the amenities of its cityscape but for location. And because it offers about the only accommodations and eating places for many miles of Mojave Desert.

Draw a circle of ten-mile radius around Barstow's main intersection and it will encompass three unusual desert-type destinations. Extend the circle to twenty miles and you add four more.

First there are two places for a briefing in town. Take the Central Barstow exit from the I-15 freeway and go north on Barstow Road. The first place, immediately on your left, is the Mojave River Valley Museum, jam-packed with mementos of the past and a source of information on history and natural history. Their "Tour of Local Historical Places," if available, has some fascinating data.

Then north down the street is the Bureau of Land Management's Barstow Way Station, another museum and information source. Of particular interest is an annotated map, *High Desert Recreation Resources Guide,* that locates and describes places mentioned below.

Barstow is a railroad town, and three of its highlights are rail-oriented. One right in town is Barstow Station, a collection of rail cars converted to shops and eating places and usually bulging with travelers from the highway. Another is the vast Santa Fe classification yard off Main Street west of the town center; it has a visitors' observation point. The third is the grand old Harvey House hotel, fenced off but partly visible up close, just across the bridge over the river and tracks — a prime restoration candidate.

The ten-mile radius includes Rainbow Basin, a brightly colored eroded rock formation north of town. To the northeast is Calico, the former mining town restored as a tourist attraction, but now a county park — though the nostalgic shops, train ride, and mine tour still operate. To the east is Daggett, a somnolent but fascinating old settlement that includes the ruin of the 1880 Stone Hotel, once a stagecoach stop; the 1890 Alf blacksmith shop (not open to the public), where the great twenty-mule-team freight wagons were built; and other relics.

Extending the radius another ten miles takes in Yermo to the east. It has an appealing old rail station where often the huge Union Pacific Centennial engines park — the biggest things on rails today. Farther east, the Calico Dig early man site is now a park operation, with guided tours to a campsite believed to date from 50,000 years ago. (Take the Mineola Road exit north from I-15.)

North of Barstow there is often land-sailing activity on dry lakes reached by the Copper City Road. And there are both petroglyphs to be seen and rocks to be found in the Inscription Canyon-Opal Mountain-Black Mountain area. (Be sure to inquire about road conditions before setting out on backroads to these places.)

CAMBRIA, *Prelude to the Hearst Place*

This trip offers the quiet pleasures of beach and blufftop sea encounter and poking around in little towns, along with Hearst Castle as chief destination. That state-owned extravaganza doesn't need description here except to state the ground rules: You can see it only on a guided tour; there are three different tours at various times; you need reservations; and you should allocate at least half a day.

This is a coast of hills and rocky cliffs — though nothing like monumental Big Sur to the north. Begin at Morro Bay (see Chapter 12) on Highway 1. Aim for Cambria for overnight, and plan to stop at Cayucos, with its beach and fishing pier, and Harmony, inland in a sheltered valley. Both have clusters of shops, eateries, and such, fitted into nicely restored buildings.

(San Simeon, another brief settlement, north of Cambria, has an atmospheric old landmark general store — Sebastian's — and a fishing pier and deep-sea fishing boats. You're well into salmon territory along here.)

A string of five state beaches between Morro Bay and San Simeon offers places to wade, swim (if you don't mind the cold water), go rock or surf fishing, and have a picnic.

Despite the road map, Cambria is not right on the coast. It's almost two towns, an older area upstream in an arroyo protected from ocean weather, and a newer, larger section below that contains shops, galleries, even a little theater with an adjoining pub. One store has a large, if specialized, following: The Soldier Factory, for its miniature military figures.

There are several restaurants. One motel is in town, while three others are on Moonstone Beach Drive, out by the shore. Note that in summer you may need reservations for rooms as well as for a castle visit weeks in advance.

THE DELTA, *Houseboat Cruising Waters*

Hidden below the levees that lace the flat land some distance inland from San Francisco Bay is a network of hundreds of miles of waterways frequented by ocean-going freighters (in the ship channel), yachtsmen, fishermen, water-skiers, and a special breed of escapist vacationers who inhabit houseboats. This is the delta of the Sacramento and San Joaquin rivers.

You can sail in or launch your own boat at a number of marinas, or even rent a boat. But the typical rental is more of an ark than a boat, shallow of draft for shallow water and not awfully subtle in response. It is not difficult to handle, even so, though some boating experience is a definite asset.

These squarish craft can be comfortable enough for a family or a group of, say, six friends to spend several days on. Some became quite luxurious in the decade of development when houseboating really caught on in the 1960's. The big operators in Stockton, Antioch, Bethel Island, and other access points advertise widely in newspaper travel sections; you can usually compare several sets of costs and equipment features.

The days afloat are leisure at its best. There are few goals along these sluggish tidal passages: a pleasant anchorage, maybe, or shade where you can tie up along the bank (it gets hot in summer). Your voyage can be almost aimless, though you should keep track on your chart well enough to be able to get back to the right place.

The scenery is reminiscent of the Mississippi, with an occasional small river town, or a marina or resort, or a landing for gas and supplies. You sun on the top deck, or dive overboard on occasion, or drop a fishing line. The chief events are landings and meetings with other craft in passing. Nothing seems urgent.

JULIAN, *Back-Country Gold Town*

This is an adventure into mountains of the San Diego back country to the town of Julian, a little over 4,000 feet high. It lifts you into mountain air, sharp tanged compared to the soft atmosphere of the coast. And it offers rarities in California: snow in winter, color in fall (the oaks are memorable), and surprising color in spring — when pinks and yellows and the vivid blue of mountain lilac flower complete a tonal orchestration that starts with complex chords of greens.

The most delightful thing about old Julian is the twelve-room, bathroom-down-the-hall Julian Hotel, vintage 1887. It's a real hideaway place.

The town around is tiny and homespun, and about it the atmosphere of its 1869 mining boom still lingers. You can visit a gold mine, the Empire, on C Street. And go see the delicate Victorian Witch Creek School, moved in to house the library, and the Julian Museum, open on weekends. And be sure to come for Julian's famous plant exhibits, the wildflower show the third week in May and the weed — or dried plant — show the last week in August.

The countryside around is bountiful with apples, pears, and peaches, so there are blossoms in spring and fruit in late summer and fall — along with such goodies as jellies and fresh-fruit pies.

A further culinary institution is down the road at Santa Ysabel: Dudley's Bakery, which brings in customers from great distances for its fresh wares. Otherwise, that village is notable for having one of California's little-known inland missions, founded in 1818 (though the present building dates from 1920).

The mountain neighborhood also contains Cuyamaca Rancho State Park, with its forest-ringed meadows. And just down the Banner Grade, which descends the steep east slope, the vastness of Anza-Borrego Desert State Park spreads out.

OAKLAND, *East Bay Metropolis*

San Francisco so dominates the Bay Area that it's easy to overlook the fact that other cities have some perfectly civilized facilities, too. Oakland, just a short drive across the Bay Bridge (or a BART ride), is one of them.

The city has been enriched in recent years by two striking additions. One of them is the snazzy Paramount Theatre on Broadway, downtown, a restoration of a gaudy 1930's movie palace as a performing arts showcase.

The tile-clad Paramount is next to a tile-clad I. Magnin store of equal Art-Deco extraction. Both are part of a Broadway that has been upgraded by landscaping and new building, following the placing of the BART line underground.

The other addition was the Oakland Museum. Designed by architect Kevin Roche, it is almost a non-building and therefore fits gently into the cityscape. A superb system of roof gardens and steps, it also happens to contain halls that display selections from the definitive collection of California art on the top level, and history and natural science on lower levels. A feature of the latter is a remarkable walk through the biotic communities of the state.

The museum faces Lake Merritt, the great open breathing space of water and park in the center of things. It's a fine place for a stroll, also used heavily by cyclists (before 11 A.M. on weekends) and joggers. The landmarks on the southwest are the Municipal Auditorium, the squat tower of the Alameda County Courthouse, and the tower of Kaiser Center; the remainder is mostly residential.

Around the lake, clockwise from the southern end, you encounter a boathouse, Children's Fairyland (all the name implies in a tots' playland), a bandstand, bowling and putting greens, a garden center and a cluster of gardens, a boathouse for rental sailboats and rides on a paddlewheel boat, water bird refuge, an eating terrace at Lakeside Inn, an aviary complex that includes a large hemispherical free-flight cage, a natural science center, a pergola out of the early part of the century. That gets you to the upper end of the eastern arm of the lake. The return is mainly a walk beside the water.

Elsewhere in town, there are performances by the Oakland Symphony and summer musicals in the Woodminster Amphitheatre. And on a slightly less lofty plane, some dashing spectacles at the Oakland-Alameda County Coliseum — stadium — by the Raiders, A's, Golden State Warriors, and others.

West of downtown are some visitor attractions, two of them named for writers. One is Bret Harte Boardwalk (he once lived close by), a cluster of meticulously-restored Victorian houses turned into shops and an excellent restaurant.

Between there and the harbor is the sometimes grundgy, sometimes colorful old produce district, with a scattering of restorations, retail shops, and small restaurants.

Then where Broadway meets the waterfront is Jack London Square. This is several blocks of shops, restaurants, yacht basin, and sea-wall activity. It has a focal point near the mast of the cruiser *Oakland* in Heinold's First and Last Chance Saloon — verifiably a Jack London hangout — and the writer's Yukon cabin, shipped back and reassembled.

Then, to tie this all together, take the scenic drive, marked by signs to be seen at the square. (You can pick up a map of it at the Chamber of Commerce office at 1939 Harrison Street; 451-7800.) The drive includes Berkeley and Alameda as well as Oakland.

SACRAMENTO, *Capital Exploring*

A rectangle of one square mile — two miles long by a half mile wide — contains most of the attractions of this city, which is somewhat underrated as a visitor destination.

The rectangle extends from the Sutter's Fort restoration at Twenty-Seventh Street roughly west to Old Sacramento State Historic Park on the bank of the Sacramento River. And it reaches from H Street (where at Sixteenth Street stands the Victorian Old Governor's Mansion) roughly south to P Street, which is south of the landmark Crocker Art Gallery.

That creates a perimeter for a driving tour. Within it is a smaller, more concentrated rectangle — Fifteenth to the River and I to N — feasible for an exploration on foot.

Sutter's Fort may be a good place to start, for this is where Sacramento started as New Helvetia in 1839. From the fort Captain John Sutter ruled his agricultural domain like a barony — until he lost it when gold seekers overran the land a decade later. Now part of a state historic park, the fort has been restored as a microcosm of frontier life. And next to it, on the side opposite the entrance, the State Indian Museum displays an interesting collection of artifacts from many Indian groups.

Then you might do the pedestrian section of town, starting with the Governor's ex-mansion — now also operated as a museum by the State.

Next, go west a block to Fifteenth and south (past the Italianate Memorial Auditorium) four blocks to Capitol Park. This is forty acres of lawn and a tree collection that amounts to a botanical garden. It has specimens from the world over, plus a cactus garden, a rose garden, and a camellia collection.

The graceful capitol building occupies the center of the park. You can tour it, following completion of work to make it earthquake resistant. Its portrait gallery and the 1913 Arthur Mathews paintings inside the dome are noteworthy.

West of the capitol stretches the mall, starting with a state office building on the north and the State Library opposite; look inside it to see the Maynard Dixon mural.

The government-lined mall is of passing interest. The K Street pedestrian mall to the north, through the shopping district, is livelier. (Note its tram as a way to return, if you parked near the Governor's Mansion. It reaches to the theater-meeting spaces of the Community Convention Center at Fourteenth.)

At Seventh you can go north to Pioneer Hall (at 1009) and the displays of the City and County Historical Museum.

Then west on J Street you come to the striking buildings of the big Chinese Cultural Center. Between Fourth and Fifth, it has a temple, garden, offices, shops, and restaurants.

Beyond that, between the freeway and the river, is the 28-acre restoration area of Old Sacramento.

This is striking for having been built up over existing ground after the level of the river rose because of the great volume of gravel washing down from hydraulic mining along

Sierra foothill streams. Streets and buildings from the mid-nineteenth century have been restored or rebuilt, and the buildings house working enterprises, not just museum displays. The railroad museum, though, is one, and it has some marvelous old engines and cars.

The other signal attraction nearby is the E. B. Crocker Art Gallery, on Third south of O Street. Here an 1873 mansion of unusual opulence houses an unexpectedly good collection of Old Master drawings along with its European and American painting.

Then if you want to go walking, bicycling, horseback riding, even boating or fishing, or play golf, Sacramento has an unusual chain of parks for these activities. The American River Parkway is a linkage of more than twenty miles of park land beside the river from Nimbus Dam and the Folsom Lake State Recreation area down to its meeting with the Sacramento River. The property includes the California Exposition (state fair) site east of I-80 freeway.

SAN JUAN CAPISTRANO, *Harbor and Valley*

Judging from the crowds, as many people as swallows come back to Capistrano on March 19, the traditional day of return. Even on other days of the year the place gets a good deal of traffic.

This is partly because of the song about swallows, partly because it is a good halfway point on the highway between Los Angeles and San Diego.

But there's more to San Juan than most stopover visitors see, and enough to its segment of lower San Juan Creek to warrant close inspection. The short vacation described here will range from the sea close by to San Juan upstream to Caspers Regional Park.

This is Dana country, from Richard Henry Dana's *Two Years Before the Mast,* written in 1840. One of the famous incidents took place here, near San Juan, at what came to be known as Dana Cove. In it, Dana tells how the company of the brig *Pilgrim* sailed cattle hides over the cliff to the beach below to be loaded aboard the ship.

Today Dana Cove has been absorbed into a small-craft harbor, but a little clifftop park at the foot of the Street of the Blue Lantern in the town of Dana Point memorializes the hide-tossing. Dana Point Harbor spreads out down below, and where its central road reaches the outer edge you can see a bronze statue of the young seaman-author.

The harbor is a park, with picnic tables, lawn, even a small beach with a small fishing pier. It is also the setting for marinas, boat-launching ramps, party-boat docks, restaurants, shops, and motel. This is one place to stay in an area of scarce accommodations (others are to be found in Dana Point, San Juan Capistrano, and nearby in South Laguna and San Clemente).

Adjoining the harbor on the east is Doheny State Beach, straddling the channelized mouth of San Juan Creek, with camping as well as day-use facilities.

A roadside bike lane heads inland from the harbor on Del Obispo Street several miles to San Juan, for a car-free approach to town. (Then north of town, Camino Capistrano — formerly Highway 101 — is now a pleasant, lightly-traveled road for several miles, much used by cyclists.)

San Juan, of course, has the mission as centerpiece. Its old stone church is as majestic a ruin as you can find, its Serra chapel is an unusual combination of frescoed adobe with a rich Spanish baroque altarpiece. All around, trees create a garden atmosphere far more lush than anything of Spanish days.

Out in town there are several blocks of shops, some of excellent quality wares, some in old adobes. And restaurants. One occupies an early adobe, one is in the handsomely-restored Capistrano train depot (where Amtrak will stop at the wave of a flag).

Other antiquities are visible but not publicly open, notably the restored Victorian house of Judge Egan right on the main street. Some not readily visible show up on Sunday afternoon walking tours. Notice of them is posted around town; or call at the chamber of commerce for information.

Caspers Park, about 8 miles up the canyon from San Juan, is a 5,500-acre chunk of former ranchland preserved as a hikers' and horseback riders' park — with camping and picnic facilities. It's a great place to see some unspoiled countryside, still beyond the growing edge of the metropolis nearby, of sycamore-lined stream, meadow, oak woodland, and chaparral.

SAN LUIS OBISPO, *Interlude of the Past*

Like many Spanish settlements, an inland town for an essentially seacoast area, San Luis is a repository of a past that began two centuries ago with a mission. Its 1794 successor today forms the heart of what has become a small metropolis.

There are other adobes about, and other gems from early times: The brick store of Ah Louis, for example, from last century, and the cast-iron facaded Sinsheimer Brothers store. The wooden St. Stephen's Church (a reconstruction) and the stone Carnegie Library — now the County Museum. A handful of Victorians and a 1930's Art-Deco county building and a movie theater. There's even a Frank Lloyd Wright office building.

This catalog of antiquity is assembled for the motorist and the dedicated walker in the form of a Path of History. The route appears both on a map, available at the county museum and the chamber of commerce, and as a green stripe on the pavement of central streets.

It all centers about a delightful park and plaza in front of the mission and along San Luis Obispo Creek — a principal asset of the city, though long overlooked. The park is lawn and trees up above, a riot of growth down along the steep banks. And there are pedestrian bridges. Restored factories — cigars, a creamery — along the creek create some of the most atmospheric settings for shopping and eating.

San Luis is on the coastal slope, so it relates easily to the sea. The towns of Morro Bay and Pismo Beach (see Chapter 12) are both part of its orbit. So are the state park holdings nearby: Morro Bay State Park, Los Osos Oaks State Reserve, and Montaña de Oro State Park.

The Morro Bay park is described in Chapter 12.

Los Osos Oaks is a remarkable landscape, a little more than seven miles west of U.S. 101 on Los Osos Road. Here dunes from the edge of the estuary beyond are covered with venerable oaks fifteen centuries old, festooned with Spanish moss and embowered in ferns. Their contorted forms are strangely moving, and their dwarf size — rooted as they are in ancient sands — makes them eerie and dramatic natural bonsai.

Montaña de Oro is a park for hikers, out seaward of the town of Los Osos. Along three miles of craggy coast, it has properly minimal development. It offers a variety of Bishop pine, culminating in a long view from the high point of Valencia Peak.

SAUSALITO: *Looking Back at San Francisco*

Sometimes it's worthwhile crossing the Golden Gate to Marin County just to get out of fog and into the sun. On other clearer days it's worth the trip just for the stirring view back at the San Francisco skyline.

Or maybe you'd just like to spend a day or two in such a quaint and curious setting as precariously-perched Sausalito — what a Mediterranean village might look like if they used wood there to build houses.

There are no grand hotels, but a handful of small, well settled-in places spot the Sausalito hillscape. These include the fine old Alta Mira, the Sausalito Hotel, and the Casa Madrona, each offering amenities of view or seclusion. (Otherwise, it's motels in towns nearby or along Highway 101.)

Sausalito is more of an atmosphere than a place to do things. It has one busy major street at the foot of the cliffs, Bridgeway, location of most of the shops and such restaurants as the superlative Ondine, out where you can enjoy the view of bay and city to the fullest.

North on Bridgeway there is an arid, industrial stretch — interesting, though, for having the Corps of Engineers' vast model of water flow in the Bay and Delta. Beyond is the houseboat moorage, then the highway.

The shore along here fronts Richardson Bay, and one of its agreeable features is the Audubon Sanctuary off Tiburon Road. Unmistakably signaled by a well-cared-for upright Victorian house, it is mostly marsh. In late spring the nesting of egrets is the best part of a show that includes migrant birds heading north.

Ahead, Tiburon Road leads to Tiburon, a nucleus of activity at bayside, including a ferry over to San Francisco, mainly for commuters, and another to Angel Island. The waterfront is the site of several restaurants, of which The Dock, The Windjammer, and the more costly Caprice are some of the best-known. A little inland, a row of former arks from Belvedere Cove is Tiburon's most unusual feature. They're now converted to dry-land use as shops of more than usual character.

Angel Island, across turbulent Raccoon Strait, is a state park these days. Free of car traffic (you can reach it only by ferry), it is a fascinating place for a walk, bicycling (bikes are for rent), and a picnic. Again, the view of San Francisco is dazzling, rising behind the hard-nosed silhouette of Alcatraz Island.

Elsewhere in the neighborhood, the prime recreation goal is the out-of-doors, grouped mainly in two clusters of parks. One includes Mt. Tamalpais, a commanding vista point favored of hikers in the state park of the same name, and Muir Woods, closest redwood grove to San Francisco. Two more park properties adjoin this pair, reaching over to the coast at Stinson and Muir Beaches.

The other cluster is the Marin Headlands-Golden Gate National Recreation Area. Comprising the windswept hills and wild beach north of the Golden Gate, it evokes some of the brooding, treeless stretches of the weather coast of Ireland.

SOLVANG, *Sun Field*

"Sun Field" translates the name of the village that started in 1911 as a settlement to prepare Danish immigrants for their new country. The place flourished and went on to become that rarity, a popular visitor-attraction town well off the main highway (which is U.S. 101, about three miles west).

It's a stage set for a cheerful scenario of Danish pastries and Royal Copenhagen blue plates, of imported sweaters and wooden shoes, of Karlsberg beer and enough delicatessen items for a week of picnicking, of soft pretzels over the counter and *aebleskiver* (pancake balls) to eat for breakfast or anytime.

So what if the windmills that punctuate the skyline don't actually grind grain or pump water? And what if the medieval theater at one corner of town produces a Theaterfest of summer Shakespeare? The slight incongruities seem minor when the crowd is having a good time and taking center stage anyhow.

They stroll streets as alive with pedestrians (in season) as any in Southern California, poke about a multitude of shops, ride the Hen — a replica Danish streetcar at your service — and look at such sights as the transplanted Danish Lutheran Church and the Old-California Mission Santa Inés, both not far from the center of town (nothing in Solvang is far from the center of town).

The summer surge of visitors crests at Fourth of July with a good-fun parade and again the third week in September with Danish Days — a costumed song and dance and food fest nostalgic of the Old Country.

Solvang is the hub of the Santa Ynez Valley, but the valley is worthy of exploration in its own right. You will transit its upper part if you take the San Marcos Pass route (Highway 154) in from Santa Barbara. You come over the mountains and down past Lake Cachuma, with its park and boats, and then the horse farms. Beyond are side trips to Ballard, noted for its authentic old one-room schoolhouse, and Los Olivos, site of a real stagecoach inn from the old days. A little farther out is the handsome big Firestone winery near the junction of Zaca Station and Foxen Canyon Roads. And little Santa Ynez, close to Solvang, has a handful of antiquities "downtown."

Down the valley from Solvang are more horse farms. On Santa Rosa Road you encounter a park among old oaks and across the valley the state-restored Mission La Purísima Concepción. Then you reach the famed flower fields around Lompoc — a varicolored quilt that heightens in intensity as spring advances. Finally, at the foot of the valley you meet the sea at Surf — a name on the map but not a town.

Gondola cars soar above Mammoth's slopes, snow-covered until June

Chapter 14:

Top 10 Ski Resorts

THIS CHAPTER IS basically a list. The grading of anything as subjective as a ski vacation is nearly impossible, so I have fallen back on presenting those places that have the most of things. This means the major ski areas that draw the major crowds, particularly on weekends and the big holiday seasons. It may not mean they are the best when the traffic gets congested, parking becomes a problem, and the wait in line for the lift gets to be long.

Still, the big ones offer the greatest choice of facilities. In the listing I have assumed the presence at the site of places to eat, lodges and warming huts, and equipment rentals, and the availability of nearby accommodations.

I mention special facilities such as cross-country instruction and snow-making equipment, where appropriate, though a number of places have snow play facilities without making a point of it and often such other services as baby-sitting. Note that in this competitive field an equipment list can go obsolete fast as operators add facilities. Such situations as the drought of recent memory encouraged installation of snow-making machinery, for example, though not everyone wanted to emphasize that addition.

In the following directory, the number of lift facilities constitutes an index to the scale of the operation (the term "others" includes T-bar, poma lift, rope tow, and other devices). The size of the longest run is also an index of scale, and the altitude has something to do with both amount of snow and length of season. Mammoth, for example, is remarkable for its altitude reaching up to 11,000 feet and its season that starts early and lasts (God willing) into June.

I haven't tried to include an index of proficiency required of skiers at each place. Most operators will assure you they have a mix of perhaps a fourth for novices, half for intermediates, and a fourth for skilled skiers — or similar percentages. One, Sugar Bowl, weights its evaluation of its slopes as fully half for advanced skiers, and Alpine Meadows gives the figure as 40 percent, but all the rest regard about half the terrain as intermediate.

The list is grouped according to the three major areas of (mostly) reliable snow. For a note on skiing at Yosemite see Chapter 6.

LAKE TAHOE

Here the combination of a network of access roads, and excellent supply of year-round accommodations, and an extended upland in the snow-catching elevations has nurtured the largest collection of ski resorts in California. All are within in easy weekend reach of the Bay Area.

Apart from the ski facilities, the state parks of the Tahoe area conduct an interesting program of snow activities that includes ski touring, guided snowshoe hikes, and even ice fishing. For information, write to Sierra State Parks, P.O. Drawer D, Tahoma, CA 95733, or telephone them at (601) 525-7232 during office hours on weekdays.

ALPINE MEADOWS, Box 1334, Tahoe City, CA 95730, (916) 583-4232. Take highway 89 south from Truckee. Open mid-November to mid-May. Downhill and cross-country instruction and cross-country trails. Nine double chair lifts, 4 others. Longest run is 2 miles, altitude ranges from 7,000 to 8,700 feet.

HEAVENLY VALLEY, Box AT, South Lake Tahoe, CA 95705, (916) 541-1330. Off Highway 50, south of the lake. Open mid-November to mid-May. Downhill ski school, snow-making equipment. Tram, 15 double chair lifts, 9 others (tram also operates in summer). Longest run is 7 miles, altitude range is 6,100 to 10,150 feet.

HOMEWOOD, Box 165, Homewood, CA 95718, (916) 525-7256. Off Highway 89, west of the lake. Open late November through early April. Has downhill ski instruction, snow play area. One quadruple, 2 double chairs, 6 other lifts. Longest run is 2 miles, altitude range is 6,200 to 7,900 feet.

NORTHSTAR AT TAHOE, Box 129, Truckee, CA 95734, (916) 562-1111. On Highway 267, southeast of Truckee. Open late November to late March. Has downhill and cross-country instruction and cross-country trails. Six double chairs, 1 rope tow. Longest run is 2½ miles, altitude range is 6,400 to 8,600 feet.

SQUAW VALLEY USA, Box 2007, Olympic Valley, CA 95730, (916) 583-6985. On Highway 89, south of Truckee. Open late November through May. The big one, with downhill and cross-country instruction and cross-country trails, indoor ice rink. There is also a novice area at Papoose in the valley (Box 2008), (916) 583-3451. Gondola, triple chair, 20 double chairs, 2 pomas. Longest run is 3 miles, altitude range is 6,200 to 9,000 feet.

SUGAR BOWL, Norden, CA 95724, (916) 426-3651. On old Highway 40, west of Truckee. Open November through May. Has downhill and cross-country instruction and cross-country trails. One gondola, 7 double chair lifts. Longest run is 2 miles, altitude ranges from 6,880 to 8,400 feet.

EASTERN SIERRA

Two ski resorts here are easier for Southern Californians to get to by car than the Tahoe complex or some of those reached via the west slope of the Sierra.

JUNE MOUNTAIN, Box 146, June Lake, CA 93529; (714) 648-7733. On Highway 158, west of U.S. 395, about an hour north of Bishop. Open mid-November through mid-April. Has downhill instruction, night skiing, snow-making equipment, outdoor ice-skating rink. Five double chair lifts and a T-bar. Longest run is 2 miles, altitude range is 7,600 to 10,200 feet.

MAMMOTH MOUNTAIN, Box 24, Mammoth Lakes, CA 93546, (714) 934-2571. On Highway 203 west of U.S. 395, about 50 miles north of Bishop. Open November through June. Has downhill instruction; three cross-country ski operations are nearby in Mammoth Lakes. Two gondolas, 16 double chair lifts, 4 others (gondola also runs in the summer). Longest run is 2½ miles, altitude range is 7,950 feet to over 11,000. Also call at the Inyo National Forest Visitor Center in town to inquire about their winter programs.

WEST SLOPE SIERRA

And here are two of the several in the Sierra south of the Tahoe cluster, reached from Gold Country towns.

BEAR VALLEY-MOUNT REBA, Box 38, Bear Valley, CA 95223, (209) 753-2301. Up Highway 4 from Angels Camp on the Ebbetts Pass road. Open late November through April. Has downhill and cross-country instruction, cross-country trails, toboggan runs and snow play equipment. Seven double chair lifts and a poma. Longest run is 3 miles, altitude range is 6,400 to 8,500 feet.

KIRKWOOD, Box 1, Kirkwood, CA 95646, (209) 258-6000. On Highway 88, the Carson Pass route, about 55 miles up from Jackson. Open late November to late April. Has downhill and cross-country instruction, cross-country trails. Eight double chair lifts, 3 others. Longest run is 2 miles, altitude ranges from 7,800 to 9,800 feet.

INDEX TO HIGHLIGHTS OF THE TEXT

Ahwahnee Hotel   60
Alisal   106
Alpine Meadows   138
Angels Camp   79
Arboretum, Arcadia   34
Auburn   80
Avalon   113

Badger Pass   62
Balboa Park   11
Barstow   123
Bear Valley - Mt. Reba   140
Beaulieu Vineyard   97
Beringer Vineyard   98
Beverly Hills   36
Briggs Cunningham
  Automotive Museum   89
Buena Vista Winery   103

Cabrillo National Monument   15
Calistoga   100
Cambria   124
Cannery Row, Monterey   45
Carmel-by-the-Sea   47
Carmel Valley   48
Century City   37
Chinatown, Los Angeles   34
Chinatown, San Francisco   23
Christian Brothers wineries   95, 98
Civic Center, Los Angeles   33
Coloma   80
Columbia   79
Concrete Wave   91
Coronado, Hotel Del   107
Coulterville   78

Delta   125
Disneyland   85
Domaine Chandon winery   96
Downieville   81
Downtown Los Angeles   32
Downtown San Diego   14
Downtown San Francisco   22
Downtown Santa Barbara   52

Embarcadero, San Diego   14
Ethnic districts, Los Angeles   34

Financial district,
  San Francisco   22
Forty-Nine Mile Drive   26
Freemark Abbey Winery   98
Fun Bus   84

Furnace Creek Inn and Ranch   106

Gamble House   35
Getty Museum   37
Glacier Point   62
Glen Ellen   102
Golden Gate Park   28
Golden Gate Promenade   25
Golden Gateway   23
Grass Valley   81
Griffith Park   39

Hancock Park   36
Harbor cruise, San Diego   15
Harbor cruise, San Francisco   25
Harbor Island   15
Heavenly Valley   138
Heitz Wine Cellars   97
Heritage Park   11
High Sierra camps   65
Hollywood   38
Homewood   138
Huntington Library   35

Indio Palms park   72
Inglenook Vineyards   97
Inn at Rancho Santa Fe   108

Jacks Peak park   49
Jackson   79
Jackson Square   24
Joshua Tree National Monument   72
Julian   126
June Mountain   139

Kartopia   91
Kirkwood   140
Knott's Berry Farm   86
Konocti Harbor Inn   108
Kornell Champagne Cellars   100
Krug, Charles, Winery   98

La Jolla   18
Laguna Beach   114
Lake Cahuilla park   72
Lion Country Safari   88
Little Tokyo   34
Living Desert Reserve   71
Lodge at Pebble Beach   109
Long Beach   114
Los Angeles Harbor   114

Mammoth Mountain   139
Mariposa   78

Mariposa Grove 64
Martini, Louis, Winery 97
Mecca Hills park 72
Mendocino 116
Mission Bay 16
Mission Beach 16
Mission Canyon 54
Mission Dolores 28
Mission La Purisima
 Concepcion 135
Mission San Carlos Borromeo 48
Mission San Francisco Solano 103
Mission San Juan Capistrano 131
Mission San Luis Obispo 132
Mission Santa Barbara 54
Mission Santa Ines 134
Mokelumne Hill 79
Mondavi, Robert, Winery 96
Monterey 42
Moorten Botanical Garden 70
Morro Bay 118
Movie World 90
Movieland of the Air 90
Movieland Wax Museum 89
Murphys 79

Nevada City 81
Newport Beach 119
Nob Hill 24
North Beach 24
North Waterfront,
 San Francisco 25
Northstar at Tahoe 139

Oakland 127
Ojai Valley Inn 110
Old Town San Diego 10
Olvera Street 34

Pacific Grove 45
Palm Canyon 70
Palm Springs 67
Palm Springs Desert Museum 69
Palm Springs aerial tramway 69
Pismo Beach 119
Placerville 80
Point Lobos 49
Point Loma 15
Presidio Park 10

Quail Lodge 110
Queen Mary 115

Sacramento 128
St. Helena 97

San Diego scenic drive 10
San Diego Zoo 12
San Gabriel Valley 34
San Juan Capistrano 130
San Luis Obispo 131
Santa Barbara beach 57
Santa Barbara Biltmore,
 Marriott's 109
Santa Barbara scenic drive 56
Santa Cruz 120
Sattui, V., Winery 97
Sausalito 133
Schramsberg Vineyards 100
Serra Museum 11
Seventeen-Mile Drive 46
Shelter Island 15
Silverado Country Club 101
Skatopia 91
Solvang 134
Sonoma 102
Sonora 78
Squaw Valley 139
Star of India 15
Sterling Vineyards 100
Sugar Bowl 139
Sunset Boulevard 38

Tahoe, Lake, winter sports 138
Tiburon 133
Tijuana 19
Tioga Pass 65
Torrey Pines Mesa 18
Tuolumne Meadows 65

Union Square 22

Vacation Village Hotel 111
View places, San Francisco 29

Wawona 64
West Side, Los Angeles 37
Wild, Wild, Wet 91
Wilshire Boulevard 36

Yosemite Falls 59
Yosemite Park and Curry Co. 65
Yountville 96

TWO COMPANION 'TOP 10' GUIDES ON "WINES" AND "RESTAURANTS"... FROM ARMSTRONG PUBLISHING CO.

"California's Top 10 Wines"
(With "Top 10" Lists Of California's Wine Country Tours And Tasting Rooms, Restaurants And Recipes, Wine Books and Winery Newsletters, Places To Stay And Things To Do, Drinks And Cheeses, Quotes And Toasts)

ISBN: 0-915936-09-7 / $4.95

"California's Top 10 Restaurants"
(And 266 Other Great Places to Eat That Don't Rip You Off!)

ISBN: 0-915936-04-6 / $4.95

EASY MAIL ORDER
For *each* book, mail check for $6.25. Price includes UPS delivery, sales tax and handling. Address to: Armstrong Publishing Co., 5514 Wilshire Blvd., Los Angeles, CA 90036.

PHOTO CREDITS:

Francis Coleberd - 20; Larry Dunmire - 99; Walter Houk - 8, 13, 17, 30, 40, 50, 55, 66, 82, 92, 112, 122; Mark Miller - 63; David Muench - 58, 74; Hugh Tolford - 136; Herald Toutjian - 117.